Retirement Income Planning:
The Baby-Boomer's 2017 Guide to Maximize Your Income and Make it Last

Written By: **Mark J. Orr, CFP® RICP®**

Certified Financial Planner™

Retirement Income Certified Professional®
and a fee-based Investment Advisor Representative

Visit my website below to see retirement videos and BLOG posts. Join My Retirement Income Planning Email list for more financial planning and retirement tips too.

SmartFinancialPlanning.com

2nd Edition -- Copyright 2017

D0291334

Preface

Writing a book about retirement income planning is not an easy task. There are literally 1,000's of potential situations and personal circumstances, income goals, legacy aspirations, fears and legitimate risks that virtually all Americans will face over a possible 30-45 year retirement.

My purpose here is not to provide a one-stop answer for every near retiree in America. No book could do that. But my purpose is to give the reader a very broad and encompassing, yet highly easy-to-read resource that will provide you with many different aspects of planning your retirement.

Whether you choose to be a "do-it-yourselfer" or want to work with a professional advisor, this book will give you plenty of insights to make sure that either you or your advisor is properly covering the all of the bases. You'll learn the most important questions to get answered as well.

You will read about strategies for maximizing Social Security and pensions, minimizing income taxes and investment risk, fighting long-term inflation and planning for a very long life.

Before making nearly "unfixable" mistakes, learn about all of your retirement income options. Read, learn and enjoy... Mark J. Orr, CFP® RICP®

Thank you for purchasing this book.
Up to $1,000 a year of royalties from this book will be donated to The Rotary Foundation

What's Inside This Book – Table of Contents

Introduction

Mount Everest is the world's tallest mountain and has lured thousands of climbers to challenge reaching the summit. Folks spend years preparing for the feat.

Still, nearly 300 of the world's best climbers have died trying - due to lack of preparation or perhaps just plain old BAD LUCK. But making it to the top is just half of the battle. Did you know that most deaths have NOT happened on the climb up to the peak... but they occurred on the decent!

To help in making it to the top and back safely most climbers hire a Sherpa. These experts have made this dangerous climb dozens or 100's of times before. So what does this have to do with retirement?

People spend years preparing for and climbing towards their retirement goal. Those are the saving years. This phase stops when you reach the peak and retire. Your final decent starts the day your paycheck STOPS -- and the income withdrawals BEGIN.

That's the perilous distribution phase where too many retirements fail. As a professional retirement income planner I have designed many, many retirement income plans and that experience is the basis for this book. Do you have a retirement Sherpa to ensure your success?

Here's an interesting question for you. What is another way to describe retirement? It is being "unemployed" for the next 30-40 years. Only Social Security, any pensions and your life savings will get you through the next two to four decades.

Success in retirement has less to do with assets... and most everything to do with INCOME! It is income that will separate the have's from the have not's – especially after the first 10-15 years of being "unemployed". It's all about building a long-term sustainable and rising monthly cash-flow.

In my mind, there are 4 basic boxes that pre-retirees (and those who are currently retired) will belong to. Each person will fall into one of the first two -- as well as one of the second set.

The first box is for those who are financially prepared to retire. For whatever reason, they were good savers, good investors, built and sold a successful business, have a great pension, inherited money, etc., etc. They have enough money so that they will have to try pretty hard to ruin what would otherwise be a prosperous and long retirement.

On the other side of that spectrum is those, who for reasons of their own making (poor decisions), or just plain old bad luck again, have not been able to prepare for retirement as well as they wish they had. And of course, there is the whole spectrum of those folks in between those polar opposite ends.

The third box (and first of the 2ⁿᵈ set) is the do-it-yourselfers (DIY) who have never used a professional financial advisor (and may never will). And the opposite of that person is the client of one or more financial advisors over their working years and investing life.

Both the DIY person and the advisor's client may or may not have had much investing success over their working years. Or either of them could have done very, very well over that time.

But I will tell you something that is a fact and widely known in the Certified Financial Planner community – that there is a world of difference between saving for retirement... and relying on your savings for a regular paycheck for the rest of your life. These are two very different skill-sets indeed.

As I tell my personal clients all of the time, "success in your retirement has less to do with your accumulated assets and everything to do with having a written, understandable and conservative lifetime income plan". It's all about cash-flow!

Having accumulated assets is one thing, but how do you optimally turn those savings into an income to last your (and perhaps your spouse's life). That "pile" of savings has to last for what will likely be a very long retirement.

As I've said, another way I describe retirement is: "30-40+ years of unemployment". The paychecks stop rolling in. There are no more sick, personal or vacation days. No more company benefits. This is no time to be making financial mistakes or forgoing financial opportunities that will mean the difference between retirement success and failure.

Except for those who, by whatever manner has a big stockpile of cash/investments, it is an income and income tax plan – not the level of savings that will separate the have's from the have nots in retirement over the long haul.

Even folks who have amassed a great amount of assets can make some major or expensive mistakes in not making the most of those savings, through ignorance, greed, poor decisions and income tax-inefficiency.

If you are currently married, have you ever considered what happens when one of you passes on? When two Social Security checks go down to one (you get to keep the largest check and lose the smaller one). That's a major change to cash-flow that is completely unavoidable.

If you have a pension, how secure is that pension? I wouldn't want to rely on a teacher's pension if I taught in Detroit, or a policeman's pension in Chicago or one of dozens of jobs in hundreds or villages, towns, cities, counties and states that have underfunded pensions. The same could be said about 1,000's of public and private corporations. I'll write more about potential concerns of a pension later on in the book.

There is no easy way to fix this for millions of Americans who are relying on what was supposed to be a guaranteed lifetime income.

Did you know that even the "timing" of your retirement will have a very substantial bearing on its success? Joe retired in 1974 and with inflation over the next 25 years, for every $1,000 per month in income he needed back then, he needed $3,379 a month in 1999... to live the same exact lifestyle.

But Joan, who retired in 1986 with $1,000 per month income needed only $2,064 dollars 25 years later (2011) to keep up with inflation. Inflation had a 37% less impact on Joan than Joe. How big a role will Inflation play in your retirement?

The same effect of retirement timing holds true with the sequence of investment returns and even prevailing interest rates as is does with the inflation examples given above.

What about government policy risk? For example, Congress just changed some of the rules for Social Security filing which cost many of my current and future clients up to $50,000 or more that we had planned on getting! Are you ready for some additional potential government "means testing" for benefits?

The purpose of this book is to help you ask the right questions and make the best financial decisions regarding Social Security, pensions, and mitigating investment, interest rate and longevity risks, liquidity and government risks and the adverse effects of both higher inflation and taxation.

Saving for Retirement

So let's get started!

I think it would be pre-mature to jump into a book about retirement income planning without first having mentioned anything about "SAVING" for retirement.

This is where preparation comes in. We have very much control over how much we save each month, where we save it, how long we work before choosing to retire.

One of the questions I frequently ask people that I come into contact with is, "are you 100% sure that you are going to have a great retirement... or do you have some doubts"?

A good many of those folks tell me they have doubts. Some have small doubts and others know they are in trouble. And of course, some people have no idea and don't even know how to go about answering that question. Has anyone ever asked you?

By the way, for those who believe they are in trouble of out-living their retirement savings and then completely relying on Social Security, there is a pretty common reason they want to explain to me. What do you think is the biggest reason that the people who have doubts is? It was because of too much debt over their working lifetime. I'm not judging, but this just makes common sense, doesn't it?

Over my many years of being a professional financial planner, I have found that one of the biggest reasons why many folks have not saved enough for retirement, is that they carried too much debt – especially "bad" debts. Too much debt equals big monthly debt payments which hamper the ability to save for retirement.

What do I mean when I say "bad" debt? I mean virtually all types of non-mortgage debt. Credit card debt, consumer debt, personal lines of credit, student debt, etc.

Not that having a mortgage debt and monthly payment that is oversized in relation to your income is good, but at least you get a tax deduction. And usually that debt has a relatively low interest rate too.

Do these comments make sense to you? Is bad debt the biggest reason that you or someone that you care about hasn't been able to save enough to retire the way you/they dream of?

Although this is way beyond the scope of the book, what would you think if I told you that a part of my financial practice is to help people get out of ALL debt (including a brand new 30 year mortgage) in about 9 years or less... WITHOUT changing your current lifestyle one bit. You still get to enjoy your life.

The only caveat is that although we do this every week for folks across the country, I am not a magician and cannot help someone who earns $1 and then spends $1.10.

If becoming totally debt-free sounds like something you (or your relative/friend) would like to explore further, just give me a call and I could show you how our powerful strategies would perform for you – at no cost or any obligation.

OK, let's move on and continue with saving for retirement.

Most people save for retirement in their employer's plan at work, like a 401(k), 403(b) or 457 plan. Some folks save on their own in an IRA, SEP IRA, SIMPLE IRA, or invest in real estate or something else.

One big mistake I see many small business owners make is that they don't save outside of their own business. In other words they put everything back into their business and don't have a separate retirement plan. Many of those folks think that they will be able to sell their enterprise when they retire.

Unfortunately, for 10,000's of business owners, that will not likely be the case. All too often, THEY are the business.

And when the owner leaves, there's not much left to sell. Certainly not for anywhere near what they might be planning on.

Of course, there are many exceptions where a business has been built to the point where it does not depend on the owner being there every day, and the business can be sold for a substantial sum of money.

If you own a business, it may be a very smart idea to speak with a professional business broker who could give you some guidance of how "sellable" your business is now and what you will need to do to increase its value to a potential buyer down the road.

The next section is written for those who are still saving for retirement (or perhaps to teach your adult children).

Tax-Postponed vs Tax-Free Savings

But let's go back to the traditional retirement plans that were mentioned above. There are two basic types of qualified retirement plans: 1) the traditional IRA, 401(k), etc. where the IRS allows you to deduct the contribution on your taxes today, and defer your taxes until you take the funds out in the future and 2) a ROTH IRA or ROTH 401(k) where you contribute after tax dollars (no deduction today) but assuming you follow the IRS rules, income taxes will never be due in the future.

Most people think that a tax-deferred retirement plan saves taxes. I believe they NEVER save any taxes. They only "<u>postpone</u>", not only the tax payment, but the calculation of the tax bill into the future.

Which is best? Well, if you think taxes are going to be lower in the future than they are now, then a tax-postponed plan may be right for you. But if you think that tax rates will be higher (and/or tax brackets will be lower) in the future, I'd rather pay the tax today – at known rates. ROTHs also do not have Required Minimum Distributions (RMDs) which I will discuss later in the book. Nor do distributions from ROTHs affect the taxation of your Social Security checks!

If you have years left before retirement or have young adult children that are just getting started in their career, I would highly recommend them contributing to a ROTH (foregoing the tax deduction today) when they are in the lower earning years of their career (and lower tax brackets with mortgage interest deductions, child exemptions, etc.) and protecting them from paying higher taxes on a bigger account balance in retirement.

Here is an example which shows how you might not save taxes with a traditional IRA, 401(k) etc. In fact, the IRS becomes your investment partner. They "own" part of every dollar in your qualified retirement accounts (IRA, 401(k), 403(b), plans).

Let's say you contribute $10,000 a year to your 401(k). If you are in the 30% marginal tax bracket, you'll "save" $3,000 a year in income taxes. Over 30 years, you will have "saved" $90,000 in taxes ($3,000 per year x 30 years) on your $300,000 of total retirement contributions. Now let's fast forward to your retirement.

The way I see it, you really did NOT save a single dime in taxes. You ONLY "postponed" paying them. Accountants and the IRS calls this deferring taxes. Those small deductions that you get now (delaying taxes due)... will be long forgotten when you eventually MUST take your money out in retirement (at age 70.5) and potentially pay a much larger amount to the I.R.S.

So let's assume your 401(K) does fantastically well and that tax rates do not rise! If you take $50,000 out of your taxable 401(k) or IRA in retirement and your marginal tax rate is still 30%, you'll pay $15,000 in taxes. Remember, the IRS "owns" part of these accounts!

In just your first six years of taking retirement income from your 401(k), you will have "repaid" the I.R.S. ALL $90,000 of your so-called "tax savings". That's exactly what you actually "saved" in taxes during the whole 30 YEARS of making retirement contributions.

And if you take annual retirement income for more than six years, your 401(k) or IRA it could cost you a FORTUNE in taxes. You see, if you live 30 years in retirement, you could pay $450,000 in TAXES on withdrawals from your 401(k). That's right; you could pay one and a half times as much to the I.R.S. in taxes than you actually CONTRIBUTED ($300,000 in this example) to your 401(k). Think about that.

Do you HATE taking on new debts? Do you hate owing cash to anyone? I believe that with 401(k)s and IRA's you are just building up a huge debt (future taxes) to the I.R.S. that will have to be paid. In effect, the I.R.S. is putting a "tax lien" on your IRA, 401(k), 403(b) or any other tax-qualified plan.

Now a lot of you may be saying to yourselves, that my taxes will be lower in retirement. That could be – especially if you plan on living on less income during your golden years.

With the National debt at some $20 TRILLION dollars and growing at some $3 million a minute most people believe that income taxes will have to go higher. Add the more than $51 TRILLION dollars in un-funded Social Security, Medicare and Medicaid promises, and each American citizen's share of the debt is some $200,000 and counting.

It is my personal opinion that income tax rates are actually "on sale" right now. They may never be lower again. So if you have traditional IRA's, or a 401(k), 403(b), I believe you might want to consider converting a portion of these account to a ROTH. Is your tax-preparer advising you about your options?

Prior to 2013, the top federal bracket was "only" 35% but the "fiscal cliff" deal just raised that top rate by nearly 5%, so the wealthy ($400,000 net annual income or more for singles and $450,000 for joint filers) will pay even more.

On top of that, effective in 2013, a new law subjects those with high incomes (over $200,000) with a 3.8% additional Medicare "contribution" (read: tax) on ALL unearned income (interest, rents, dividends, etc.). What are you doing to combat the prospect of higher income taxes in retirement? There are even new proposals in Congress to tax dividends on stocks at your highest tax bracket rate. That failed in the "fiscal cliff deal" but taxes on dividends did go up from 15% to 20% on the wealthy (and then add the 3.8% Medicare tax and dividend income is taxed at 23.8%).

What's next? If you happen to live in California, state income taxes just went up another 3% to 13.3% for the wealthiest. What state is next with an income tax increase? Even states with no current income tax might begin taxing you. Many folks want to take practical steps now to prevent even potentially higher income tax bills down the road.

Would you bet on lower taxes during retirement? What tax deductions will you have then? Will your house be paid off when you are retired? If so, there goes your mortgage interest tax deduction. Any children still at home? No. Well there goes some of your personal exemption deductions.

I suggest that you pay taxes once (on your paycheck) and then never pay them again on your savings. Even with the 2016 election results, the hope for lower taxes might pan out. But tax laws can potentially change every 2 years and I still believe that with our nation's debt – taxes will have to go up.

However, if your employer offers an attractive contribution match, I almost always suggest contributing as much as you can to take full advantage of the company match. That's free money. But I wouldn't contribute a penny more there.

And you'll see later on in the book that we'll want "some" taxable retirement money in the future to take full advantage of (at least as of the current tax code) of standard deductions and personal exemptions.

What do you do with the extra money that you'd rightfully like to put away for your future? Well many folks use a ROTH. But they have limitations. For example, the most any person can contribute to a ROTH in any year is $6,500 (adjusted for inflation). That low amount might not be enough to provide the retirement of most people's dreams.

And the IRS says that if you make too much money ($133,000 for single filers and $196,000 for married filing jointly in 2017) you CANNOT even contribute to a ROTH IRA. Many of my clients, including myself, are in that boat.

Again, where I contribute 100% of my own money for my future retirement is also beyond the scope of this book. But my first book that I wrote fully described a much more flexible ROTH IRA tax-free cash-flow "alternative".

Unlike a ROTH IRA, this alternative has no IRS contribution or income limits, has no IRS restrictions on accessing these funds at any time and comes with more benefits than a ROTH. It also allows my savings to work for me in two places at once which makes for a very powerful saving and accumulation strategy.

If you'd like to learn more about this very flexible tax-free cash-flow supplemental retirement income alternative, with no stock market risk, I encourage you to order my book.

Average Investor "Success"

Speaking of stock market risk, whether you save for retirement in an IRA, 401(k), 403(b) or even in a brokerage account, you might be interested in knowing about how the average investor has performed over the last number of years.

In 2016, the highly respected research firm DALBAR, reported their annual study that found that while the S&P 500 had returned +8.19% annually over the 20 year period ending in 2015, the average equity investor -- only earned +4.67% a year over those two decades. But the average equity investor is getting better! Over the last 30 years, the average investor lagged the S&P 500 index return by nearly 7% a year.

Average means that half of these investors did better and half did even worse. According to USNews.com, "A report on ETFs (Exchange Traded Funds) reached a similar conclusion. In 68 out of 79 ETFs, the returns experienced by investors lagged that of the ETFs themselves by over 4%".

It's the 23rd year in a row, the "twenty year DALBAR study" showed that average investors do much worse than the market (the last 30 year periods were even worse). Besides their "chasing" last year's "hottest" mutual funds and getting "hot tips" from well-meaning friends, why do some investors fare so badly?

The answer is that some people can be way too emotional when it comes to their money. They tend to BUY HIGH and SELL LOW... instead of BUYING LOW and SELLING HIGH. When the stock market is crashing and they can't take seeing their losses any longer, they sell low. And when the market almost fully recovers as it always has, they forget the emotional pain of the last market drop and the actual amount of their losses, and they finally invest again or "buy high".

Of course, you might be an "above average" investor who actually enjoyed good annual returns and avoided the bear markets of 2000-2002 and again in 2008.

But while we're speaking about returns, let me show you an example about how Math Does NOT Equal Money. That's right, there is a difference between actual returns (money you can spend) and average returns! Check out a very interesting and quite popular 5 minute webinar that I recorded on my website: **www.SmartFinancialPlanning.com/math-equal-money-video**

Retirement Risks

Ok, we're at the point in this book that you bought it for – you are near or in retirement and you want to make it the best that you can. You want to optimize your assets and minimize making any avoidable mistakes that could have a profound effect on your retirement success – not outliving your money.

I have already compared retirement income planning to Mount Everest. Nearly 300 of the world's best trained and experienced climbers have died trying to make it up and down the mountain.

Most of those deaths on the mountain, the retirement "deaths" have occurred on the decent which begins the moment your paycheck STOPS --- and the withdrawals commence. Professional planners refer to this as the "income phase" of retirement. Whereas I've already written these words, this is when cash-flow is king! Cash-flow. Cash-flow.

I think the best way to move forward from here is to have a brief discussion on risks that we will all face in retirement. There are at least five major retirement risks. Some we can do a pretty good job of reducing and for some others, there is little we can do – but you should know what they are there.

Everyone knows that we are living longer and longer. My clients will tell you that I write and speak a lot about longevity.

But I only do so because it's so very important in planning your retirement. In my opinion, longevity is by far and away the largest of those 5 major retirement risks. No other retirement risk even comes close. Why?

Because the longer you live, the more likely the other major risks of inflation, investment losses, higher health costs and tax increases are to happen. That's right, the more years that you live, the higher the chances of facing each of those retirement risks (as well as others). I'll discuss each of these major risks in more detail below. But first, let me focus on longevity risk.

According to Social Security, half of all woman aged 65 today will live to or beyond age 84. But the longer people live, the more likely they are to last into their 90's. Let me repeat that because it is very important. The longer you live, the more likely you will live into your 90's!

Once that same woman hits age 84, she's likely to live another 7 plus years. At age 91, there's a 50% probability that she'll still be blowing out candles at age 96. And if you'll indulge me one more moment, at every age 96 or older there's a good shot of becoming a centenarian.

If that woman is healthy and active as a 65-year-old, the odds of a very long life get even higher. She has a 62% chance of living to age 90 and a 28% chance of living to age 95.

The statistics for men are very similar but about 3-4 years lower in ages. But as a couple, the odds of at least one of them living into their 90's start getting very big.

If you are married, this is a very important point. Once you both attain age 65, there is over a 50% likelihood that one or both of you will live to see your 92nd birthday. There's about a 20% chance that one or both of you will live to 95! Yes, 1 in 5 couples retiring at age 65 will have one of them living to 95.

And this is based on medical science and health services as they exist <u>today</u>. But every year medical science makes huge progress in fighting and preventing diseases. Based on the past, our longevity will likely continue to increase every decade.

According to a recent New York Life study of people aged 80 or older, more than half of the octogenarians living today, said that when they were planning their own retirements 2-3 decades ago, they "never expected to be still living now".

They didn't expect it but look where they are today. It's my job to not only expect it... but to actually plan for it. When I design retirement income plans for my clients, I like to run them out until age 100 (especially for a couple!). Now to be fair, most of my clients will NOT live that long but I suggest that you or your advisor does the same.

So if we agree that longevity is the mother of all of the other risks since the longer we live the more likely we'll experience all or some of the other retirement risks.

Let's continue with the risk of investment losses. Investment losses when you are spending down your assets is very different than investment losses while you are saving for retirement (the accumulation phase).

There have been 9 recessions and bear markets since 1957. That works out to one about every 6.33 years on average. We had 2000-2002. The last one was in 2008-2009.

As I update this book in December 2016, we're over 7 years since the last one. So is the next one going to be in 2017, 2018 or 2019... and how bad will it be? How long will it last?

Whenever the next one is, I can tell you one thing. Based on the past, if you and/or your spouse are going to live some 20-30 years or more in retirement, you may well experience another 4 to 6 of these bear markets and recessions (along with extended periods of very low interest rates again). Are you fully financially and emotionally prepared for this?

If you are only going to live ten years in retirement, investment losses (risk) isn't as big a deal – especially if a good portion of your retirement income is based on Social Security or some other type of pension.

I'll be writing about sequence of returns (which goes hand in hand with investment loss risk) later in the book. It's such a big deal that it deserves its own section. But for now, just know that at what points during your retirement would you suffer from heavy investment losses, is going to have a major impact on whether you outlive your money (ouch!)... or your money outlives you.

Rising health care costs. Similarly, the longer we live, the more likely we are going to have medical expenses that Medicare might NOT cover. And one of those BIG potential expenses that Medicare does not cover is Long-Term Care. The older we get, the more likely we are to suffer from Alzheimer's and dementia.

But let's forget about potential long-term care costs and just focus in on normal aging medical expenses. Many people think that Medicare will pay about all of one's potential health care costs in retirement. This couldn't be further from the truth.

Did you know that although Medicare Part A premiums are "free", that you'll pay in excess of $100/month (taken out of your monthly Social Security check) to pay for Medicare Part B premiums. And the higher your income the more costly Medicare Part B premiums are. So that's over $1,200 a year right there.

But Medicare does not pay all of your health expenses. You'll have deductibles and co-pays, and don't forget out-of-pocket prescription and other costs. Unless you pay for a Medigap policy (which fills in many of the gaps of Parts A and B). Although I believe that having a Medigap policy (or an equivalent) is vital protection to your assets and peace of mind, they are not cheap.

A couple could easily spend $3,000 to $5,000 (or more) a year on these policies. And even then, you'll likely still have out-of-pocket medical costs.

Most people agree that medical inflation has been and will likely continue to grow faster than regular inflation – consumer price index (CPI).

Every year the big mutual fund company, Fidelity, does a study and the results were highlighted in a Forbes magazine article on 10/07/2015:

"A couple retiring this year, both age 65, should expect to spend an estimated $260,000 on health care in retirement, according to Fidelity's 2016 Health Care Cost Estimate. That's present value, after-tax money you would need at age 65, sitting in an investment account, earning 4% after-tax going forward.

The article continues: "What if you're single? A male retiring this year at age 65 and living to 85 needs an estimated $130,000. A woman retiring at age 65 and living to 87 needs an estimated $145,000. (Because the assumption for life expectancy is different for men and women, you can't cut the couples' estimate in half; women need to save more.)

The $260,000 couples' estimate is up from $245,000 last year. There are two main reasons for the jump: updated mortality assumptions and increasing medical and prescription drug costs. "Increasing drug costs is something everyone is keeping an eye on," says Sunit Patel, senior vice president, Benefits Consulting, Fidelity Investments who worked up the estimates.

The "updated mortality assumptions" above is another way of saying – we are living longer. Those enormous figures do NOT include any costs for long-term care – which could easily cost $60,000 per year in 2017! They are made up of insurance premiums, co-pays, deductibles, and uncovered expenses.

And believe it or not, the longer we live, the more likely we will be subject to higher income taxes to pay for the trillions of dollars that our government has put on its "credit card" for our children and grandchildren to deal with. At some point, someone will have to pay the piper!

Whenever I ask someone whether they think tax rates are going to be higher in the future or lower, what do you think the most common answer is? It's nearly unanimous – most folks think taxes are going to go higher – not lower. But what most people think doesn't matter – what do you think?

The top marginal tax rate has been getting closer to its historical average of over 50% as I described earlier in the book. Of course, there's not enough "rich" people to handle getting all the revenue needed to eliminate deficits, fix Social Security, Medicare and Medicaid, fight terrorism and pay off over $20 TRILLION in debt. So the Congress will very likely have the IRS tax the middle class even more.

Despite the 2016 election results, I think taxes will have to go up across the board eventually...but that's just my personal opinion of what is going to happen. It's simple mathematics.

Whether we get to a 50% or higher top tax rate or not, the other moving part of our tax bill is "tax brackets". Congress can increase tax revenue by lowering the tax brackets that would put all of us in a higher marginal tax bracket – even if they do not rise tax rates!

They could also start "means testing" to reduce our net Social Security checks or raise our Medicare premiums even higher. Means testing could also mean certain people pay more on capital gains.

In fact, Congress has not changed the provisional income calculation since 1984. Provisional income calculates how much of your Social Security checks are subject to taxation. By not changing the provisional income levels to keep up with inflation, many millions of Americans Social Security checks have been taxed, that would not have been back in 1984.

And don't forget about inflation risk that will cause costs to rise faster than our retirement income. Inflation is normally under-reported by the government – but we all know better.

Most people fail to take inflation into account when planning on their retirement income. That is a huge mistake.

It doesn't matter what income you start with, but let me give a quick example here. If you want to live on $70,000 (including Social Security) in your first year of retirement, at just 3% inflation, in 10 years you will need to have income of $94,000 to live the same way as you did the first year you retired.

In 20 years, instead of $70,000 of spendable income, you will need $126,427 (after-tax) to live the same lifestyle as you did in your first year of retirement.

OK, so I keep writing about planning for a 30 year-long retirement. After 30 years, at 3% inflation, you will need $169,908 of after-tax income to live the same lifestyle as you did when you started retirement. Even at only 2% average inflation over a 30 year retirement, your costs of living would have gone up from $70,000 to $126,795. That nearly doubled your annual income need.

Like all of the other risks, if we only live 10 years in retirement, we don't have to worry too much about inflation.

So again, the longer we live, the more likely we are to face these and any number of risks in our retirement years. All of the risks: investment losses (bear markets and recessions), higher taxes, inflation and medical costs, - are all exacerbated by the longer number of years we spend in retirement (or being "unemployed" as I called it earlier). Longevity, longevity, longevity.

Social Security Income

For most readers, Social Security will play a substantial role in providing retirement income. It's so important for so many people that I wrote a book about it in 2013 called **"Social Security Income Planning: The Baby Boomer's Guide to Maximize Your Retirement Benefits".** And when Congress changed the laws, I made the relevant changes to the book and published it again in January 2017.

So although I am not going to repeat the 132 pages in that book (which has received great reviews from readers on Amazon.com in both paperback and KINDLE versions), I will highlight many of the major points and filing considerations here. But if you are looking for in-depth knowledge about your Social Security filing options, I'll make a "plug" for getting that book.

But let me begin by stating the overall premise of my book which was repeated in a quote I gave to the USA Today on November 4th, 2015 shown below:

ill highest 35 years of earnings, no
rt matter when those years occur,"
h he says.

DON'T DECIDE IN A VACUUM
A Social Security filing decision
ti should not be made in a vacuum,
e says Mark Orr, author of *Social*
- *Security Income Planning: The*
i. *Baby Boomer's Guide to Maximize*
e *Your Retirement Benefits.* "The
- decision on when and how to file
- for Social Security should be
• made as part of the overall retire-
• ment income plan with your fi-
• nancial goals, life expectancies
• and financial fears in mind."

That's it, the most important takeaway from my book is written in that sentence. More so than the explanation of how Social Security works, the filings considerations, the advanced filing strategies, the taxation of benefits, etc.

Although this book is more comprehensive than just focusing on Social Security income planning, I guess that I would make the same point: Don't make your retirement income decisions in a vacuum. All parts of your retirement income plan need to work together.

That includes Social Security strategies, pension planning for those that have one, 401(k) and 403(b) rollovers to a IRA's, potential ROTH conversions, investments, income taxes, legacy planning, etc.

But let's get back to Social Security basics. There are a few terms that you need to know. Full Retirement Age (FRA) is the age at which you can get 100% of your Primary Insurance Amount (PIA).

Full Retirement Age (FRA) is based on the YEAR of your birth:

The Year You Were Born	Your Full Retirement Age is:
• 1943-54	66
• 1955	66 and 2 months
• 1956	66 and 4 months
• 1957	66 and 6 months
• 1958	66 and 8 months
• 1959	66 and 10 months
• 1960 and later	67

So your year of birth determines your FRA – the age (including those extra months) that you will receive your full PIA.

Your PIA, is the amount that your Social Security statement shows you will get, if you wait until your FRA to begin receiving benefits. Now the amount on your Social Security statement is an approximation. You will not learn your exact figure until you actually file for benefits.

You probably already know that you can begin taking Social Security benefits at age 62. However your monthly benefits will be cut by at least 25% if you start receiving your benefits when you turn 62. In other words, you will only get 75% of what your full benefit would be if you wait to begin benefits at your Full Retirement Age. That reduction will carry through the rest of your life.

Taking early Social Security could cost you (and perhaps your spouse too) many $10,000's if you live to into your 80's.

The other aspect of taking it early, is that the Cost of Living increases (COLA's) are based on your check amount. So if the COLA is 3% one year the actual increased dollar amount you will get will be smaller. For example, if your full PIA was $2,000 a month and you took early benefits at age 62 with a 25% reductions, the 3% increase on $1,500 would only be $45. But the 3% COLA on $2,000 would be $60.

That may not sound like much, but over the years the increases compound much faster and greater on the larger amount. And over time, the monthly checks will be very different. COLAs matter!

Just like there is a "stick" for taking benefits early, there is a "carrot" for delaying benefits until age 70. For each year one delays starting Social Security beyond their FRA, Social Security gives you an 8% delayed credit. So if you FRA is age 66 and you wait four years to begin benefits, your initial check will be 32% larger than your PIA (plus annual COLA's).

Waiting to file until age 70 is not the right thing for everyone to do, but it should certainly be worth seriously considering for a married spouse with the largest benefit.

Someone with a $2,000 PIA at their FRA of 66, would get $2,640 ($2,000 X 1.32), plus COLA's for their first check at age 70.

Let's look at breakeven – looking at taking a 25% lower check at age 62 or waiting until age 70 (getting those 8% delayed credits from FRA at age 66).

Bill took early benefits at age 62 with a PIA of $2,000, so he'll start getting $1,500 a month then. Let's assume the average COLA is 2%. At age 70, his check would have grown to $1,767 a month or $21,204 a year.

Nancy, who was born on the same day, waited to begin her Social Security benefit until reaching age 70 to take advantage of the 8% delayed credits. Her first check will be $3,093 a month or $37,116 a year. That's a 75% larger check.

No it is true that Bill got 96 more checks since he started collecting benefits eight years earlier. At 2% COLA's he'll have already received $149,332 from Social Security.

Assuming average COLA's at 2%, at age 78 Nancy will have collected more money from Social Security than Bill. In this example, that is the breakeven year. That year she will collect $43,488 in benefits while Bill will collect $24,852.

Let's assume they both live to age 84. At that point Bill will have received $516,064 in total cumulative benefits while Nancy will have gotten $641,892. That's nearly a $126,000 advantage for delaying – assuming they both live to that age.

Obviously if Bill passed on before age 70, he was much better off by taking those 8 years of benefits (although if his benefits were larger than his spouse's and she lived to age 84) the results would have been the same as if he lived that long. I'll discuss spousal, divorced and widow benefits next.

And the longer one lives, or larger their PIA and/or the larger the COLA's along the way, the bigger the cumulative difference will be.

Now we'll briefly discuss spousal benefits. Should a spouse not have enough work history (with FICA payroll deductions) to have their own PIA, Social Security will allow that spouse to get 50% of the other spouse's PIA if that non-working spouse waits until their full retirement age (FRA). If that spouse wanted to begin Social Security payments at age 62, then that person would only get 35% of the spouses PIA (not the 50%).

And no, there is no 8% delayed credits for that non-working spouse to delay benefits until age 70. In fact, there is no benefit to anyone to delay taking benefits beyond age 70. So everyone that can get Social Security should be getting checks by age 70.

This situation is typically a housewife who has no work history outside of the home or a PIA that is less than 50% of their spouse. Social Security is absolutely gender neutral, so a man can get spousal benefits based on his wife's PIA.

There are also benefits for divorced spouses, assuming the marriage lasted at least 10 years, the person looking for spousal benefits is at least 62 and is not currently married to someone else. Your former spouse has to be age 62 but does not have to have filed for benefits yet.

Assuming the above, divorced benefits work the same way as spousal benefits – but would go-away upon your remarriage.

Likewise there are survivor benefits for widows and widowers. The deceased spouse much have had a 10 year work history (their 40 credits) and the marriage must have lasted at least 9 months (unless the cause of death was an accident). You must be at least age 60 (unless disabled when the required age is 50.

One more thing about survivor's benefits. You will must not have remarried (unless you did so at age 60 or older)! Survivor benefits work on a different formula which is beyond the scope of this book (as well as a full description of Social Security income planning).

But what is important to know here, is that when a spouse dies, there will no longer be two monthly Social Security checks coming in. There will only be one. You get to keep the largest check and lose the smallest one.

So if you go back to the Bill and Nancy example above, if Bill was married, his spouse would continue getting his checks (assuming it was bigger than her own).

Two checks dissolve into one check – the largest one!

Let's get back to Bill and Nancy. With the breakeven age of 78 in that example, it is HIGHLY likely that one or both of them will live to that age or older. So whether it is Bill or his wife, there is still a very strong reason to consider delaying benefits for the good of the couple.

For a much more in-depth understanding of Social Security, including my story of the Early's, the Waite's and the Best's which show how you can save $10,000's of taxes by using some savvy filing and investment strategies, I highly recommend getting my other book.

I'll tease you with a chart of their "taxable incomes" – all with getting $80,000 a year of income between Social Security and IRA's etc.

Take a close look at the next chart. Which taxable income from age 70 onwards would you prefer?

In other words, would you rather pay taxes on the income that the Early's or the Waite's have to report to the IRS and pay taxes on... or the Best's?

Is tax planning part of your retirement income plan yet? If it isn't yet, does it make sense to ignore the potential of saving tax dollars? A tax dollar saved, is a dollar earned.

Age	The Early's	The Waite's	The Best's
	Taxable Incomes For Each Couple		
62	$66,150	$80,000	$72,000
63	$66,150	$80,000	$72,000
64	$66,150	$80,000	$72,000
65	$66,150	$80,000	$72,000
66	$66,150	$80,000	$72,000
67	$66,150	$80,000	$72,000
68	$66,150	$80,000	$72,000
69	$66,150	$80,000	$72,000
70	**$66,150**	**$33,950**	**$17,500**
71	$66,150	$33,950	**$17,500**
72	$66,150	$33,950	**$17,500**
73	$66,150	$33,950	**$17,500**
73	$66,150	$33,950	**$17,500**
74	$66,150	$33,950	**$17,500**
75	$66,150	$33,950	**$17,500**
76	$66,150	$33,950	**$17,500**
77	$66,150	$33,950	**$17,500**
78	$66,150	$33,950	**$17,500**
79	$66,150	$33,950	**$17,500**
80	$66,150	$33,950	**$17,500**
81	$66,150	$33,950	**$17,500**

82+   and so on thereafter until the loss of one (the smallest) Social Security check at the passing of the first spouse.

I don't know about you, but I prefer the Best's tax scenario! In most cases, getting there takes planning in advance of retirement. However, it's well worth the effort.

Although the next two Social Security topics do not get a lot of press, you should know about them if you will have pension income from a job in which you (or your spouse) did not pay FICA taxes while working there. So I'll briefly mention them here. If one or both could apply to your retirement, you'll need to learn much more about them.

The **Windfall Elimination Provision** (WEP) came into existence in 1983. The WEP provision only affects those retirees who have earned a pension from a job where NO Social Security taxes (FICA) were withheld and also worked in a job(s) "with substantial earnings" where Social Security taxes were paid. For example, many local and state government agency employees do not have Social Security withheld from their paychecks. That could mean millions of baby boomers could be affected... and not even know it. NOTE: Military pensions are exempt from WEP reductions. Thank you for your service!

Despite what your annual Social Security statement may say your PIA is, if the above applies to you, you will likely be hit with the WEP reduction when you retire. However, you will have no way of knowing if and how much this provision will reduce your monthly Social Security check by... UNTIL you actually file for benefits. Talk about a surprise when you least expect it!

Why wouldn't this potential reduction show up on your annual benefit projection statement? Because the Social Security Administration has no idea that you have a pension from a job where you did not have FICA taxes withheld. In 2016, the biggest reduction to your PIA allowed by the WEP was about $428 per month. The WEP maximum reduction for 2017 hasn't been published yet (perhaps $434ish??).

The **Government Pension Offset** (GPO) works in a similar manner to WEP, but it also affects spouses and survivors who otherwise qualify for Social Security benefits... but have their OWN government pensions (lump sum or monthly) and have not contributed into the Social Security program via paying their own FICA taxes.

In these situations **where GPO may apply, the spouses will have their spousal Social Security benefits reduced by up to two-thirds**.

Now let's move on to a filing strategy that may apply to married, divorced (with a marriage that lasted at least 10 years) and divorced people might be able to use to maximize their Social Security income. Again, I'm not going to repeat the pages and pages devoted to this in my book "Social Security Income Planning" but you need to be aware of it.

On November 2, 2015 President Obama signed the Bi-Partisan Budget Bill. The stated primary purpose of this bill was to increase the Federal debt limit -- so the Social Security rules have changed!

In this Bill, Congress included Section 831 titled "Closure of Unintended Loopholes" which effectively phased out two powerful Social Security claiming strategies – "File and Suspend" and filing a "Restricted Application".

This bill made the single largest change to Social Security since the Citizens Freedom to Work Act of 2000, which first enabled both of these savvy filing strategies.

As I'm writing this book, the "File and Suspend" provision is dead and buried. Nobody can ever use this strategy again.

However, for anyone who had reached age 62 (or older) during 2015, you are grandfathered in and, if this strategy is appropriate for you, you can file a "Restricted Application for Spousal Benefits" once your turn Full Retirement Age (FRA). If you were not age 62 or older in 2015 (like me) then we are out of luck as this filing strategy will not be available to us.

Once a spouse reaches their FRA and is eligible for a spousal benefit based on his or her spouse's earnings record (PIA), he or she can choose to file a "restricted" application for spousal benefits, while delaying applying for their own retirement benefits based on his or her own earnings record (their PIA) in order to earn 8% delayed retirement credits.

Let's look at an example of this strategy in action. Joan files for her Social Security retirement benefit of $2,450 per month at age 66 (based on her own earning's record). Her husband Peter wants to wait until age 70 to file and benefit from 8% delayed credits. At his full retirement of age 66 Peter applies for spousal benefits (while restricting his own benefits) based on Joan's earnings record (since she has already filed for her own retirement benefits)

Since Peter receives 50% of Joan's PIA ($1,225 per month) right now (while she is getting her full PIA now as well). He can delay applying for retirement benefits based on his own earnings record (which is $2,466 per month PIA at full retirement age) so that he can earn 8% delayed retirement credits and increased COLA's.

At age 70 Peter will switch from collecting a spousal benefit to his own larger worker's retirement benefit of $4,060 per month (32% higher than his PIA at age 66... plus COLA's assumed at 2.8% per year).

There are many benefits to this strategy since it not only increases their combined household income right now (Peter got over $58,800 in extra Social Security income while waiting for his own benefits grow until age 70), but it also enables Joan to receive a much larger survivor's benefit in the event of Peter's death. Of course, if Peter outlives Joan, he will get to enjoy his own larger benefit for as long as he lives.

I know what you are thinking: "that's awesome!" Why don't both spouses file a Restricted Application on each other? But that is against the rules (both before and after the new laws went into effect).

Pension Income

Although for most folks in their 40's and 50's, pension plans are a thing of the past, there are still a number of people who are counting on receiving retirement benefits that their employer has promised. Some of those promises will be kept in full. But here's the truth about many of the rest of the pension plans that so many Americans are counting on.

The Government Accountability Office (GAO) has continued to warn current and future retirees that the Pension Benefit Guaranty Corp.'s (PBGC) financial assistance to multi-employer plans continues to increase, threatening the financial solvency of the fund and therefore, its guarantees to retirees.

Think of the PBGC as similar to what the FDIC is to banks – an added level of protection but with much less financial strength, backing or power.

The Guarantee fund is supposed to cover and provide a minimum retirement income guarantee to more than 10 million workers and retirees. But since 2009, PBGC's financial assistance to the troubled retirement plans has increased dramatically, primarily because of a growing number of pension plan insolvencies.

These pension plan insolvencies were caused by both very poor investment returns and too low levels of contributions to the pension plan from the employer.

By 2017, the PBGC expects the number of pension insolvencies to more than double, which will further stress the insurance fund. PBGC officials said that financial assistance to retirement pension plans that are insolvent or "are likely to become insolvent in the next 10 years" would likely exhaust the insurance fund within the next 10-15 years.

If the PBGC insurance fund is exhausted, many retirees will see their benefits reduced to an extremely small fraction of their original value because only a reduced stream of current insurance premium payments will be available to pay income benefits to retirees.

According to MSN Money, nearly 80% of the private pension plans covered by the PBGC are underfunded by a total of some $740 billion. That's nearly three quarters of a TRILLION dollars' worth of promises made that are likely not to be fully kept.

The news is even worse among the nation's largest companies. It's hard to believe, but only 18 pension plans offered by companies that are part of the Standard & Poor's 500 are fully funded.

That works out to less than 4% of the biggest public companies in America that are financially ready to keep their full promises for their employee's retirement. That's pitiful and most folks have absolutely NO IDEA how bad it is and how potentially perilous their retirement may be.

According to the PBGC, over 1,400 companies shut down their pension plans in fiscal year 2011, compared with 1,200 in during 2009. An additional 152 pension plans failed (meaning they were terminated without enough money to pay promised benefits) and were taken over by the PBGC.

Again the PBGC itself, which is funded by employer-paid insurance premiums, is running a $26 billion deficit. It is being held together by "duct tape" in the eyes of many people in-the-know.

I've already mentioned government pension funds here as well. And the PBGC does NOT cover these types of pension funds.

There are hundreds of towns, cities, counties and even a few states that have promised more than they will likely be able to deliver to both past and current employees.

If you are fortunate enough to have earned a federal pension you should have no worries. That should be as good as gold!

According to a report by the State Budget Crisis Task Force, public pension funds (cities, towns, counties and states) are underfunded by at least $1 trillion. To begin to close that funding gap, 35 states have already reduced pension benefits for their employees, and half have dramatically increased worker contributions to their plans.

Three forward-thinking states -- Georgia, Michigan and Utah — and 1,000's of municipalities have implemented what is called "hybrid plans" that include defined contribution plans (which are similar to 401k's), that shift some investment risk to workers. Expect more and more public pension funds to follow that lead each year.

The bottom line is that even though you are "counting" on a company or government pension (or even a company or government retirement health plan) in the years to come, you might consider figuring out how secure that "promise" will be (and a promise is all that it really is).

Any pension plan or health plan can be frozen, shut down or altered, changing how much you can expect in retirement.

To find out how secure or underfunded your own pension plan is, simply request that information from your HR department and carefully READ and review the annual benefit and funding statements that your plan is required to provide every year - so you can gauge its health.

Anything below 80% funding is cause for real concern and perhaps a very good reason to seriously look at taking a lump sum (and run!) if it's offered.

Taking a lump sum has its pros and cons (like everything else in this world). You can control the investment and perhaps enjoy a much higher income and have potential inflation protection (most pension income amounts are fixed for your life).

Or you could take the lump sum and then buy a guaranteed annuity income stream from an insurance company which is likely in much better financial shape than your employer. I would certainly caution against taking a lump sum and putting it in the stock market – with no guarantees whatsoever!

Many of my client's choose this path due to better guarantees, the potential for rising income most years and to keep control and access to their principal.

Again, everyone's situation is different and you should seek advice from a highly qualified and experienced financial advisor.

Putting an Income Plan Together

OK, we've gone over a number of important issues that everyone should know before they even think about trying to combine, Social Security, pensions and their savings towards an income plan that will pass the longevity test -- so we are not at the mercy of inflation and investment risks, rising health care costs and the likelihood of higher taxes.

Let me ask you a question. On any new thing that you have ever tried to learn, were you great at it right away? For example, would you have called yourself a proficient golfer the first year or two of learning the game?

Or how about cooking? Home repair? Becoming a parent? There was no owner's manual on that one. I know I made a ton of mistakes and had a deep learning curve on this one!

Think about anything new that you tried to learn in your past... and how long or difficult it was for you to master it?

Just like most things in life, there is a learning curve on any new skill. Only a small percentage of us are immediately proficient in any new area.

Most folks only retire one time. They've got one chance to make it as good as they can. Sometimes mistakes can be fixed without too much damage, other times, that's not the case.

Although no book or adult education class can truly prepare most people to plan the next 30+ years of their life, what you will read in these pages, will at least help you be aware of some important things that you might not know about.

At least financial advisors that specialize in retirement income and distribution planning (vs. accumulation) have done this before. In addition to specialized training, they probably have years of practice (on other folk's retirements!).

So certainly there has got to be some benefit and added advantage of using a professional for such an important endeavor as planning for a 30+ year growing income stream using all of your available resources (Social Security, pensions, savings, home equity, etc.) -- especially if you don't feel (and probably rightly so) 100% capable. This is where a retirement income Sherpa can make all of the difference.

Wade Pfau, Ph. D., CFA is a Professor of Retirement Income in the Ph.D. program at the American College. He holds a doctorate in Economics from Princeton University and is very well respected in the discipline of retirement income. He is the co-editor of the Journal of Personal Finance and has published many articles in financial industry journals, as well as the Wall Street Journal, New York Times, Money Magazine, etc. He is also a big contributor to the RICP® designation curriculum.

In his works, he writes about two fundamentally different retirement income philosophies which he calls: "probability-based" and "safety first". Each one has its own pros and cons. Primarily choosing one belief over the other will set the overall direction and stability of lifestyle of one's future income plan.

Those favoring "probability-based" will rely on the belief that the markets will provide large enough returns over time to compensate for the occasional yet likely negative returns. They say, "why should they give up the upside?" in return for lower returns with more guarantees? However, opponents point out that this philosophy leaves folks with both market risk (sequence of returns discussed in a moment) and longevity risk. This might mean outliving one's money and cutting lifestyle.

The "safety-first" mindset believes that, <u>at least the essential costs of living expenses</u> should be covered by guaranteed income from Social Security, pensions and fixed income annuities. These income sources are guaranteed and eliminate both sequence of returns risk and the risk of living too long and outliving your money. Lifestyle expenses "over" your monthly necessities and leaving a future legacy could be met with using market-based investments. They believe this is more prudent.

You might remember the "what's your number" commercials on TV. You know, the ones that had people carrying around big orange numbers that represented the amount they would need to retire. Their retirement savings goal. What number did you think was "your number"?

Did you have any idea where to start making your number goal? Is it $350,000? $1,000,000? Well maybe you saw an article in Money Magazine years ago that talked about the "4% rule". Here's what it is (or was) all about.

In 1994, financial planner, William Bengen developed the 4% rule. It quickly became the guiding "formula" used by both professional advisors and do-it-yourselfers for about 2 decades.

The 4% rule (or theory) says that at retirement, with a portfolio of 60% stocks and 40% bonds, one could withdraw 4% of the initial savings (and increase it by inflation every year) and the retiree would have a 90% or better chance of his income continuing for 30 years and that the savings would not be completely depleted until the end of those 30 years.

By the way, a 100% stock or a 100% bond portfolio has less than a 60% chance of lasting 30 years. Under most long-term market scenarios (back-testing), a 60%/40% worked the best.

So for example, someone with a $1 million at retirement could withdraw $40,000 the first year. If inflation was 3% that year, the second year they could withdraw $41,200. That growing income could conceivably last for 30 years until the savings and income stream would be all gone. Of course, it's even possible that your account would be larger in 30 years.

The 4% (and similar rules) fall under Dr. Pfau's "probability-based" income philosophy rather than the "safety-first". Have you already decided which mindset you favor?

If you got on a plane and the pilot announced the "good news" that there is only a 90% chance or so of landing safely at your destination, would you get off that plane?

With the stock markets at all-time highs now and the coming end to the 30 year long bull market in bonds (if you believe that interest rates will rise to more normal levels as investors will demand higher returns from riskier borrowers as government, corporate and all other types of debt continues to skyrocket) – is a 90% chance optimistic now? Who knows?

Mr. Bengen understands that as interest rates rise, the value of bonds will drop. This makes a diversified portfolio of even 30%-40% bonds more risky now. The other reason this theory is not blindly used as much anymore is largely due to something called "sequence of return" risk. I'll be writing a lot about this investment risk in the pages that follow.

Basically, sequence of return risk is that stock losses early in your retirement can have a very profound effect on whether you outlive your money or not. But for now, I'll leave it at that.

Morningstar has since (2013) come out with its 2.8% rule (replacing the much more aggressive 4%) saying that is the withdrawal rate a 60%/40% stock/bond portfolio could reasonable rely on for a 30 year retirement. That means that $1,000,000 retiree could withdraw $28,000 their first year in retirement and have that figure grow by inflation.

In an article in the Wall Street Journal in March 2013 entitled "Say Goodbye to The 4% Rule", they suggested a 2% initial withdrawal rate would more safely (a much higher-probability) bring someone successfully through a 30 year retirement.

The article states: "If you had retired Jan. 1, 2000, with an initial 4% withdrawal rate and a portfolio of 55% stocks and 45% bonds rebalanced each month, with the first year's withdrawal amount increased by 3% a year for inflation, your portfolio would have fallen by a third through 2010, according to investment firm T. Rowe Price Group. And you would be left with only a 29% chance of making it through three decades, the firm estimates." The last sentence is the real potential warning.

In May 2015 Mr. Bengen told the NY Times: "I always warned people that the 4 percent rule is not a law of nature like Newton's laws of motion". In that same article, Dr. Pfau "compared several withdrawal strategies if low rates persist or retirees face some other awful combination of events. He found that people who spend a constant amount adjusted for inflation… would have to reduce that rate to 2.85 to 3 percent if they wanted assurance that their spending would never have to dip below 1.5 percent of their initial portfolio (in inflation-adjusted terms)". That's a possible 50% drop in withdrawals.

Finally in that article, Mr. Bengen offered this advice to others: "Go to a qualified adviser and sit down and pay for that. You are planning for a long period of time. If you make an error early in the process, you may not recover."

My next question, is what if you (or your spouse) live longer than 30 years in retirement? It's a very real possibility for many folks as longevity is by far the largest of the risks in retirement.

Retiring early? By the way, some academics say that the safe withdrawal figure for a 40 year retirement plan is now only 1.5% according to some new academic research. Personally, I can't wrap my head around this low figure, but I do agree the "safe" withdrawal rate for 35-40 years must be lower than one for a 30 year retirement. That's just plain common sense.

Now many folks believe there is no way that they will live 30 years in retirement. But I'll remind you that if a couple has made it to age 65, there is a 50% probability that at least one of them will live to age 92. And a 25% chance at least one of them will celebrate their age 95th birthday (and perhaps more). And for better educated, wealthier or healthier retirees, the odds of a long life are even better.

In any case, would you rather plan on a 20 year retirement and be out of luck if you (or your spouse) lives 25 years... or plan on a 35 year retirement income stream and only live 25 years? Unless you and/or your spouse's health is not good, I hope that the answer is self-evident.

Sequence of Return Risk

This is how the mutual fund company Thornburg Investment Management defines sequence of return risk: "Sequence of returns is simply the order in which returns are realized by a retiree. The consequences of a bad sequence of returns, especially early in retirement, can mean premature depletion of the portfolio. Retirees need to avoid being in the position of having to sell during inopportune market environments." I'll add more practical value and an eye-opening example next. Given the heights of the market now, it should be a warning.

Rob Williams, managing director of income planning at the Schwab Center for Financial Research says: "When you're withdrawing funds at the same time that your portfolio is losing value, you can expose yourself to a phenomenon known as sequence-of-returns risk. The order in which investment returns occur can have a huge impact on your assets long-term if you are taking withdrawals from (or even adding to) your portfolio". The biggest risk is during the withdrawal phase.

Let me be clear that sequence of return risk is not applicable to a lump sum of assets. The risk is only dangerous while taking an income stream from your savings – particularly when the investment returns early in your retirement are hugely negative or very poor.

You've heard the expression "timing is everything". Well your Sequence of returns could work for you... or against you in taking income from your investments as you'll see below.

Here's an example of how a poor sequence of returns can destroy a long-term retirement plan. And just for "old-times" sake I'll also use a 5% withdrawal rate in the example too (so many people think that if my portfolio averages 7% then taking a 5% withdrawal rate should leave me with a larger balance than I started with 30 years from now!). That's not correct.

Let's look at actual returns of the S&P 500 index (with no fees or taxes) from 1989 to 2008. Then let's take those same exact returns and reverse the order they came in (2008-1989).

You'll notice that both sequences have the exact same average return of 8.49%. There is no difference in the average rate of return -- if withdrawals are not being taken.

The sequence of returns has no effect on a lump sum with no withdrawals. The middle column is the actual price returns of the S&P 500 from 1989 to 2008. The column on the far right is the same exact returns... but in reverse order.

Year	1989-2008 Sequence	2008-1989 Sequence
1	31.69%	-37.00%
2	-3.11%	5.49%
3	30.47%	15.84%
4	7.62%	4.91%
5	10.08%	10.88%
6	1.32%	28.68%
7	37.58%	-22.10%
8	22.96%	-11.88%
9	33.36%	-9.11%
10	28.58%	21.04%
11	21.04%	28.58%
12	-9.11%	33.36%
13	-11.88%	22.96%
14	-22.10%	37.58%
15	28.68%	1.32%
16	10.88%	10.08%
17	4.91%	7.62%
18	15.84%	30.47%
19	5.49%	-3.11%
20	-37.00%	31.69%
AVG.	8.43%	8.49%

So if we have a hypothetical account valued at $1,000,000 and we withdraw $50,000 (5%) and adjust that for inflation (we'll use a 3% constant inflation rate for all years), let's see how the two sequence of returns (the actual S&P 500 index returns plus the actual returns in the reverse order) plays out.

Withdrawals start at $50,000/ year and rise to $90,000 annually over the two decades (to combat inflation).

After only 20 years in retirement, the **1989–2008** sequence has more than supported the retirement spending and even allowed the account value to grow to over $3.1 million. The early years of good returns made this possible. The big losses came in the second half of the two decades. In this example the "probability-based" model worked out absolutely perfectly.

Continuing to take out $90,000 plus 3% inflation withdrawals is not going to pose a problem at all for a 30+ year retirement. But this is not a normal bull market I certainly would not want to plan my own retirement on a possible 20 year bull market.

Again, "timing is everything". Timing and the "probability-based" model could work for you and dramatically increase your savings... or against you in taking income from your investments so you outlive your savings. And the differences could be very dramatic with wide swings in possible outcomes.

However, the results for the **2008–1989** sequence (reverse order) are very different with the heavy losses coming in the first half of the period. The first year loss of 37% which was followed by significant (three years in row) negative returns in years 7, 8 and nine dramatically reduced the total account value to only about $235,000 at the end of the 20 years.

With an account balance of just $235,000 at the end of 20 years, there is virtually no way that anyone could take out $90,000 a year at that point and last more than 3 years before the account would run dry. In this case, the "probability-based" philosophy would not have worked out so well. In fact, it would have been a disastrous outcome for a 30 year retirement.

So the sequence of returns, while taking income withdrawals had a huge swing of potential outcomes. On the rosy side, the account more than tripled – despite taking substantial income along the way. On the opposite end of the spectrum, the account diminished by 73% and has no realistic shot of providing even a 23 year income to the retiree. The range of possible retirement income risks and outcomes are probably wider than it's ever been with the globalization of our economy. We could see high stock returns, big negative stock returns, high inflation, deflation, higher taxes and more changes in government policy (Social Security, Medicare, etc.).

Two of my friends and mentors are financial advisors David Gaylor and his partner Gary Reed. David writes a story in his book and we all use it in our educational classes teaching retirement income planning to consumers. I'm going to pass it along to my readers here – giving full credit where it's due!

It's the story of brother and sister, Bill and Jill who are three years apart in age. But all other circumstances they share are identical. The only difference is "Jill was born 3 years too late"! You see, Bill retired with $1,000,000 in 1996 and Jill retired three years later in 1999. Jill had an equal amount of savings as her older brother at her retirement. Only the "sequence of risk" is shown here – no other potential risks are factored in.

Both had heard on the radio that they should only invest in low-cost index funds (to pay virtually no fees). They were both excited about the big returns in the US stock market. In the late 1990's, everyone was making money. In fact, the indexes were lagging most of the companies in the tech sector, but they liked the idea of diversification at a low cost. Set it and forget it!

When Bill retired in 1996, he began using the 4% rule which has really became popular in the 1990's and was talked about on the radio and magazines as a "safe" way of not running out of money for 30 years. So Bill started taking income of $40,000 and increased his withdrawals by 3% constant inflation each year to keep his purchasing power equal to inflation.

Bill retired at an excellent time. Bill had very good returns in 1996, 1997, 1998 and 1999. Yes, he suffered like most everyone else in 2000-2002. But starting with those first four years, and even taking into account seven years of increasing withdrawals, his account never dipped below $1,000,000.

And during the recovery of 2003-2007, his account actually grew to nearly $1.5 million – while continuing to take income that had grown to over $55,000 a year. Despite his income growing to about $68,000 in 2014 and suffering through the 2008-2009 bear market (the worst since the depression), his account was still worth nearly $1.5 million.

Bill took out over $1,004,000 in withdrawals over those 19 years and his account actually grew by 49% on top of that! The sequence of returns happened to be on "his side". Of course it was just luck. No skill or advanced planning. Bill ended up in great shape for the next 10, 15 or even 20 years. He will have no income worries and have real peace of mind. And he'll be able to leave a nice legacy for his children, grandkids and/or charity. "Probability-based" planning worked well in this case.

Now let's look at what happened to his younger sister Jill. Retiring with the same one million dollars – but only 3 years later, her retirement picture would look very different.

She used the same 4% rule as Bill and the same low-cost index funds. But her timing of her retirement was not very good. As you'll see the randomness of the sequence of returns was not on "her side" when she started taking income in Jan. 1999 – even though the index returned 8.91% that first year. She would have been better off with "safety-first" thinking.

Losses in 2000, 2001, 2002 and then a whopping loss in 2008 ruined the long-term health of her retirement. Those investment losses, along with her $40,000 and growing distributions caused her account value to drop to just over $316,000 -- just ten years into her retirement! That's a 68% reduction from her initial one million dollars.

Even though 2008 was the last year that she suffered a loss, by continuing those growing withdrawals, by the end of 2014 her account was only valued at $283,000 – just 16 years into her retirement! With 2015 being a very "flat" year in the index, her withdrawal of about $64,000 in that year would have left her account valued at some $220,000. She "might" have only four or five years left of income before her savings is all gone.

Now Bill and Jill's story only focuses on the sequence of returns. Not changes in tax rates, inflation, health care costs or public policy. The longer one lives the larger these risks become

About a dozen years ago a "name-brand" insurance company started teaching both advisors and consumers about something they called the "Retirement Red Zone". They defined the retirement red zone as the five years right before you retire and the first 5 years of being retired. They promoted it pretty heavily and it makes perfect sense and is completely in line with sequence of returns risk.

But as we saw with Jill – those first 10 years killed her "dream" retirement income plan. I like to alter the "red zone" definition to cover 15 years, to the five years before retirement and the first TEN years of "unemployment"!

Are you a football fan? If so, you've heard the commentators talk about the "red zone" as the area within 20 yards of the goal line. The offense may have driven the ball all the way down the field and gotten close to scoring a touchdown.

But defenses get stronger in the red zone as there is less field to defend. It's harder to score in the red zone. The NFL even has a statistic called "red zone efficiency" – what percentage does an offense score a TD when they made it to the red zone.

What does football have to do with retirement? Well think of moving the football down the field as accumulating retirement savings. Then you get to the retirement red zone – the most critical time in retirement. It's the hardest to navigate and successfully "score" (being Bill rather than Jill).

And that huge insurance company was only referring to risks of investment returns during those years – but makes no mention of the other risks to retirement (mentioned above).

The "probability-based" folks focus on the 90% chance of retirement success, while those identifying with the "safety-first" philosophy focus more on the 10% chance of retirement failure – outliving your money. I believe in "safety-first" planning for your basic and essential expenses. Using the "probability-based" (getting both market risks and rewards) for fun spending and legacy with much less stress!

As I update this section of the book, the stock market (S&P 500 index) has hit new all-time high in December of 2016. Look at this chart below which shows the S&P 500 index from 1992 through June 2016. What do you see -- Bill or Jill's situation?

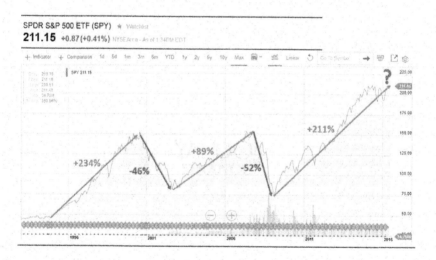

Are you in the retirement red zone? If you are, my next question to you after looking at this chart is where do you think the index is more likely to head in the next few years – continue way up... or retrace some of its huge gains for a bit? Or maybe head toward the lows of 2008 and 2009? Is this an ideal time to rely on a "probability-based" retirement plan?

US corporate profit growth (which smart accountants can make whatever they want them to be) has been slowing. Sales are not really growing either. There are many market indicators that point to another market "event". But with bond interest rates so low around the world, the market is not slowing down.

The rise in stock prices over the last eight years has had more to do with companies buying back their own stock (with borrowed money) and there being only extremely low interest paying investment alternatives... than the profit outlook of corporate America. Price/Earnings ratios are historically high.

Anyway, for a "probability-based" investor retiring in the near future, the chart shows pretty clearly that the sequence of return risk -- is probably not on their side at his point in time. Some are taking a portion of their gains made over the last 7 years off the table and placing them in the "Principal Protected" bucket (up next) that is not subject to market risk. That's probably a prudent idea.

What's the answer for somebody planning on retiring in the next one to five years? Or in the first 5-10 years of retirement?

Well I strive to fix this problem for my clients by designing a written retirement plan that shows year by year how we are going to fund their desired annual net spendable income. I'll write much more about what we call "Income Allocation" in the coming pages. It puts all of the previous pages in perspective.

I run my retirement "safety-first" practice under the guide of the four "S's": Smart, Secure, Simple and Solutions. Smart means that we don't take ANY more risk than we need, to achieve your monthly income and legacy goals.

Is there really any potential return worth losing sleep over and putting much of your life savings at risk? Is it 9%, 12% or 25%. How much risk are you willing to take... and how much risk can you afford to take? How much do you want to take?

Secure means thinking more about downside protection than a potential upside gain. Consider the "What IF you're wrong?" scenario on any number of life's variables.

Simple. People must understand their plan and why we are taking any particular step. It's got to be 100% transparent too.

And finally Solutions. Retirement planning is much more about "planning" than "products". Products just fill the need.

So planning solutions (financial products and services) must encompass the other three S's. Does your retirement strategy comply with the four S's at this point?

Retirement planning. To me, it all starts with the 3 buckets of risk and taking as much sequence of returns risk off of the table as possible. Rather than use "asset allocation" I rely on "strategy allocation" to my "income allocation" plan – so the plan has the best chance for predicable, reliable long-term success. I'll write more about both of those "allocations" later.

The 3 Buckets of Risk

When I meet a prospective new client on the phone, internet or in person, one of the first things that I like to do is talk about the 3 buckets of risk. I actually call it the 3 buckets of risk and return, but my clients just like to call it the 3 buckets of risk.

This is a very simple and easy-to-understand way for people to clearly decide for themselves, how much risk they can live with during their retirement and sleep at night.

What I have them decide for themselves is how much of their investable assets as a percentage (excluding their home) would they like to have invested in each of 3 risk/return buckets: 1) the Principal Protected bucket, 2) the Low Risk bucket and 3) the Moderate Risk bucket.

Over the next few pages, you can see the 3 buckets below as well as a brief summary of the bucket's risk/return profile.

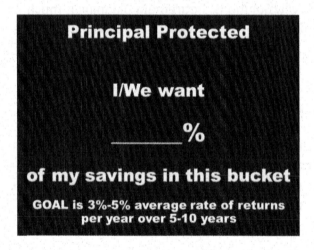

The Principal Protected bucket is exactly as it says. This is money that will never go down in value due to market risk. Many people think of CD's and 90-day Treasury bills here, and in normal times they might provide an expected return of 3%-5%, but certainly not over the last 6-7 years. CD's and T-bills have paid less than 1% over the last few years.

And it is very important to understand (especially with extremely low CD rates now) that if that "safe" money is not earning an after-tax return equal to inflation, (like CD's right now) your principal is losing purchasing power. So in this sense there could be a "real loss" -- but no losses are ever shown on your monthly, quarterly or annual account statements.

But the Principal Protected assets I typically use are products from highly-rated insurance companies (A+ rated by AM Best), or similar ratings from other independent financial rating agencies (Standard and Poor's, Moody's) that can consistently provide 3%-5% over a period of time without any risk to principal. In baseball terms, these investments are just like walks – you have no risk of getting "thrown out" on your way to first base. There is no volatility and you never go backwards.

"Principal Protected" is used in that, unlike investments (stocks, bonds, mutual funds, real estate, gold, currencies, limited partnerships, commodities futures, etc.), there is no inherent market risk to the principal. Fixed insurance products are backed by the claims-paying ability of the insurer.

Now US Treasury bonds are guaranteed to pay the stated interest and repay the full value at maturity. For example, in July 2016 the 10 year US Treasury bond yield was 1.7%. So if you bought $10,000 of these bonds, you will be guaranteed to earn that interest rate for the next ten years. And ten years from then, you will be repaid your $10,000 investment in full.

That's guaranteed by the US Government. But what is not guaranteed, is the principal before maturity nor is how inflation protected that investment may or may not be.

There is no default risk (the government can always print the dollars to pay you back). But there is investment risk if you want to sell the bonds before they mature. The value before maturity is NOT guaranteed – it could be lower or higher.

The Moderate Risk bucket (multi-asset fixed income) is for people who want or need a higher return... and are willing to take some more predictable and reasonable risks in order to earn bigger returns over time. With the 33 year-long bull market in BONDS potentially ending, in my opinion, bonds alone are not a good "buy and hold" now. They are not "Principal Protected".

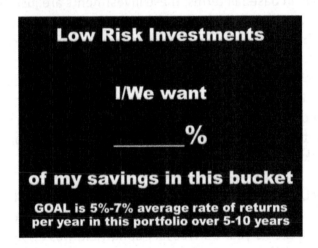

A portfolio of the investments that my firm puts into this this bucket generally provide average annual returns of maybe 5%-7% over a period of 5 or 10 years with some fairly mild fluctuations (volatility) of perhaps losing -4% to- 6% in value along the way (but that's not guaranteed). It's very possible, although not typical for this diversified bucket to lose a small percentage of your principal in a bad year, but this bucket can be pretty dependable over time.

The Moderate Risk bucket is exactly what it's named. Most savers invest in stocks, mutual funds, ETF's, variable annuities, IPO's, private placements, hedge funds, limited partnerships, etc. to attempt to earn higher returns (8%-10% or more) to compensate for much higher risk than either of the other two buckets. With historical market losses of up to -50% or more (2000-2002), the Moderate Risk bucket is usually better suited for "accumulation over time" than for monthly income.

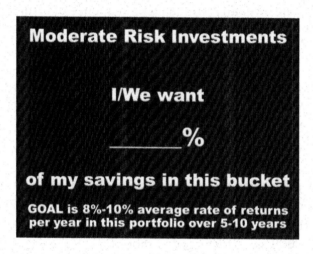

In baseball terms, this is trying to hit occasional homeruns with many strikeouts (potentially BIG losses) along the way. Over time, you might get 8%-10% or higher returns -- although the S&P 500 index returned virtually nothing during the period of 2000-2011.

That's a dozen years with nearly 0% returns (excluding about 2% in dividends). All with tremendous volatility (with large and scary losses of 40%-50%) along the way.

In fact, even including dividends from 2000-20016 the total annualized return of the S&P 500 was only about 6.6%. That's about two-thirds of what investors were hoping for (while taking substantial risks and enduring high volatility).

Taking regular income from volatile investments is not a sure thing as we saw in the section about sequence of returns.

It can either truly ruin a long and prosperous retirement... or leave your kids wealthy (with a lucky sequence of returns). During 2000-2002 the market dropped by about -40%. In calendar year 2008 the market (S&P 500 index) fell some -37%.

Drawdown is a word investors use to describe "peak to trough" drops in investment value. The S&P 500 peaked in October 2007 and hit it's trough on March 9, 2009. The actual drawdown over that time was -51%.

Why is minimizing drawdown important? As you can see from the chart below, suffering a -25% loss needs a 33.3% gain just to get back to breakeven. For the -51% loss that ended on March 9, 2009, investors needed more than 100% gain just to get back to where they were in 2007!

Please take a moment to study this next chart.

Limiting drawdown is crucial for those in the "probability-based" retirement planning mode. We saw what drawdown did to Jill's retirement income earlier. The less income you have that is guaranteed, the bigger the issue of drawdown becomes.

Percent Loss	Percent Gain
5%	5.3%
10%	11.1%
15%	17.6%
20%	25.0%
25%	33.3%
30%	42.9%
35%	53.8%
40%	66.7%
45%	81.8%
50%	100.0%

Even during 2011, a year in which the S&P 500 index price began at 1258 and ended the year at the same price of 1258 (but earning some 2.1% in dividends that year), there was huge volatility – price swings. In this calendar year alone, there were 13 periods when the price of the index went up or down by 7% or more! Thirteen times! That is a lot of volatility to withstand to only earn 2.1% of dividends – especially while drawing a monthly retirement income.

When you are in the accumulation phase, you have time to recover from (ride out) these market drops. However, many people panic and sell near the bottom, only to buy back in again near the top once they begin to forget the earlier financial pain. That's selling "low" and buying "high". Not good.

That's what many folks did – sold in late 2008/early 2009. And when the market soared +32% in 2013, they finally started to get back in. Many folks are just getting back in during 2016!

So the first thing my new clients do is tell me how much of their assets (as a percentage) do they want in each risk bucket. How much to allow them to sleep at night... no matter what is going on in the economy or the markets.

This is the first indication whether someone is more likely to primarily have a "probability-based" or a "safety-first" mindset.

There is no right or wrong answer. The only answer that matters is the one that gives you (and your spouse) peace of mind and helps you attain all of your financial goals.

Oftentimes, the husband has one set of percentages in mind while the wife has a different set that she feels most comfortable with (usually more conservative). Then it's just a matter of making a compromise they both can easily live with.

Getting the right mix (for YOU) of percentages of your assets in the right bucket is the first step in the investment process. This is an easy step for you to complete - just go with your gut feeling on what you would feel comfortable with -- no matter what is happening now, or can or will happen in the future in the stock, bond, real estate or commodities markets. But here is the strange part.

Most people's "desired" percentages in their risk buckets... are NOTHING like how their portfolios are actually invested.

It's crazy. What they say they "want" is NOT what they "have". When I do portfolio reviews for new potential clients, I find that nearly 90% of the time, the percentages they say they want in each of their 3 buckets... is absolutely nowhere near what they actually have. It's hardly ever even close!

Either their current financial advisor isn't asking the right questions or isn't paying much, if any, attention to your answers and feelings. This could be a recipe for emotional pain.

The next step in the process is to find the lowest risk (lowest volatility) investments for the two non-"Principal Protected" buckets to provide the expected returns over time to attain your goals. That's where a professional can add great value and experience (as well as provide access to certain guaranteed income investments that consumers can't get on their own).

It's my personal belief that there is more opportunity in helping my clients avoid the losses than there is in picking the winners. Reducing investment drawdown during the retirement withdrawal period should the primary goal for these two buckets -- with chasing big returns being secondary.

This way, the investor's aversion to overall risk and financial returns will be better combined to help reach their retirement objectives... and sleep at night. It doesn't have to be difficult to attain your income and growth goals. If you could get the same investment return with lower risk, wouldn't you do so?

The question is... "How much of your assets should be put in each bucket to help you reach your financial goals... while allowing you to sleep at night in virtually any market conditions?" Even if a 2000-2002 or 2008 happens again.

Sometimes one must take on a bit more risk to reach their income or savings goals at the expense of their complete peace of mind – in order to "catch up" or "make-up" for a low past savings rate... or to overcome a history of poor investing.

But investors should carefully consider taking much more risk than they need to in order to attain their financial goals and objectives. If you can't live with a certain level of risk – don't even try. If you do, you will never have true peace of mind.

Your risk/reward preferences (the 3 bucket allocation) may change over time and your choices of investments should then mirror those changes. Take a few minutes and write down how you would allocate your own risk buckets? If you have a spouse, each of you should do this and compare preferences.

Although this book is not about my personal financial practice, many people will wonder what the author does for his clients. Right now, with CD's and money market accounts not paying anything, in the Principal Protected bucket, I use 2-3 fixed annuities from very highly-rated insurers that guarantee a lifetime income for one or both spouses. Ones where you don't give up control of and access to your money... or disinherit your children from the get-go. Some have no fees!

More importantly, unlike 95% of annuities where your first check is your best check, these certain products are built to give clients real potential for increasing lifetime income. So instead, your first check... is your worst check. I like bigger and bigger checks during a long retirement to combat inflation and eliminate both longevity risk and sequence of returns risk.

Even if CD's were paying 5%-6% now, in my opinion, they could not compete with these guaranteed retirement income products. It wouldn't even be close (for lifetime income). I'll write more about these potential income solutions in the section about income allocation later.

In the Low Risk and Moderate Risk buckets, I prefer to use 3rd party private wealth managers (strategy allocation) who for the most part will go to cash when the markets are trending downward to reduce drawdown.

No manager or investment strategy works in every economic condition or market. They are human and make mistakes and mis-judgements.

Unlike "buy, hold… and pray" investment management, at least their strategy is to attempt to avoid major losses when markets crash which can add to risk-adjusted returns. Each of them have very good long-term risk-adjusted track records, but past performance is not a guarantee of future results.

Reducing drawdown is vital during the withdrawal phase as I've already discussed – especially for "Probability-based" folks.

These private wealth manager portfolios are not available to the public without an advisor. But in my opinion, a diversified portfolio using "strategy allocation" is one that has lower volatility and a better chance for long-term retirement success.

"Safety-first" minded clients with money in both these bucket know about and accept these reasonable risks --- especially when they have most or all of their monthly income needs taken care of by income sources like Social Security, pensions and guaranteed income annuities.

In the Low Risk bucket, I use a mix of 5-11 these private wealth managers to attempt to reduce portfolio volatility and provide good risk-adjusted returns.

And for the assets that most of my retired clients put in their Moderate Risk bucket, I use a portfolio of 7-12 money managers with different investment strategies. Like the managers in the Low Risk bucket, most of them will go to cash. Taken together as a portfolio, the expected drawdown and volatility could have the potential to be even lower than the market for this risk bucket as a whole.

Why take more risk than you need to in order for that portion of your portfolio to do very well? I think there is more opportunity to help protect folks from losses... than taking bigger risks than needed, in the hope to reach for gains.

How do these investments in the low risk and moderate risk buckets help do that? Again, because most of them can go to cash when the markets are trending downward. And a few of them can even profit from market crashes by going "short".

The goal in retirement income planning is to maximize the income while minimizing the risks and volatility of your investments. Less sequence of returns risk. Reduce drawdown. Does it make sense to use a lower-risk portfolio (trying to reduce the amount of volatility) in order to have monthly income stability and a high probability of long-term retirement success (not outliving your money). Less volatility could equal less stress!

That's opposed to most investor "asset allocation" portfolios that are what I call a "hope and a prayer" portfolio – possibly stuffed with high risk, highly volatile mutual funds, stocks, real estate, commodities and even "bad" bonds. More importantly, most of these portfolios do not equal the desired 3 buckets of risk percentages the investor said they felt comfortable with.

Later on, I'll write about retirement "income allocation" planning and using this "strategy allocation" instead of the typical "asset allocation" that some advisors and consumers are familiar with. Here's why I think this is going to be a critical part of your retirement success.

There have been nine recessions and bear markets since 1957 (the year I was born). That works out to one about every 6.33 years on average. We had 2000-2002. The last one was in 2008-2009. As of this revised edition in December 2016, we're gone more than seven and a half years since the last one.

Will there be one going to be in 2017, 2018 or 2019... and how bad could it be? If there is a next one, I can tell you one thing. If you and/or your spouse are going to live some 20-30 years or more in retirement, it's possible that you experience another 4 to 6 of these bear markets and recessions (along with new periods of very low interest rates again). Are you fully emotionally and financially prepared for this?

Have you spent most of the first decade of this new century, just recouping the past gains you had earned before the market dropped yet once again in 2008/2009? Taking 2 steps forward, one step back (over and over again)? I hate taking unnecessary investment losses more than I do paying income taxes!

As I update this book for 2017, U.S. stock markets are at all-time highs. With that said, the founder of Vanguard Funds, John Bogle, has stated twice during interviews on CNBC TV (2014) and elsewhere that he expects two bad bear markets with stocks dropping up to 50% in the next 10 years or so. Who can tell the future but what if he's only half right?

Warren Buffet has said numerous times that he thinks the stock market will only average in the mid-single digits over the next 10-15 years. That means he is expecting stocks to have annualized total returns (dividends and appreciation) of only 5%-7%. Who knows that the future will bring, but what if he's right on those lower than historical average annual returns?

Will the portfolio that you currently have, help weather any of these potential steep market drops and continue to provide the same and growing (inflation protected) income to supplement your guaranteed Social Security checks? Social Security and pensions are your base, but what about the rest?

Some people are predicting the Federal Reserve will raise interest rates in 2017. That's great for borrowers, but awful for bond investors. As interest rates rise, the price of bonds falls. The US 10 year Treasury bond was under 1.7% in July 2016. It's almost 2.5% in December. So in about six months, the value of that US Treasury bond declined by about 7%! Germany, Switzerland and Japan had negative interest rates in 2016 where you had to pay the government to invest in their bonds!

According to bankrate.com this morning, the best 5 year CD rate in the country is 2.1%. And to get that you really have to shop around. Most banks are offering less than 1.25% rates for a one year CD. Those interest rates are way less than inflation.

I won't go into which specific investments I use for each bucket as that is beyond the scope of this book. But it is imperative that most of my readers understand what allocations of investments they want to go into each bucket so they can sleep at night – while providing a steady monthly investment income to supplement their Social Security checks.

To me, that is the only definition of a good portfolio – one that provides the needed and increasing investment income over the next 20-30+ years while letting you sleep at night – no matter what's happening in the economy. One where drawdown and sequence of returns risk is minimized.

By the way, would you like to see how closely your desired percentages in your 3 buckets… actually match your current portfolio? You will likely be very surprised… and sometimes even very upset with your current advisor or even your own portfolio choices. Better to know the truth. If so, please contact me and I can give your current portfolio a free "risk analysis".

Now like the 3 buckets of risk, I also like to teach my clients about the 3 tax buckets. As I hinted earlier in the book with the Earlys, the Waites and the Bests, keeping your income taxes as low as possible is another important part of your retirement income plan. I'm not a CPA (and don't play one of TV), don't do client tax returns, but I do know a little bit about income taxes.

You have probably heard about these 3 buckets before, but have you actually tried to put the "right" investments into the "right" tax buckets? It can make a big financial difference over 2-3 decades of your retirement. And then I'll give you a quick course on income taxes – how to basically calculate them, etc.

The 3 Tax Buckets

There are **3 basic types of tax buckets** to hold investments or money in: 1) Taxable 2) Tax-Deferred and 3) Tax-Free. Given the choice, most folks would choose to keep the majority of their assets in the **tax-free bucket** for obvious reasons.

When I begin working with a client in their 30's, 40's and 50's, this is pretty easy to do. Nearly 100% of my own retirement savings is in the tax-free bucket. Later, I'll give you an example of how planning ahead (at least 10-15 years before you retire) can put you in the position of paying as little as 2% federal taxes on $100,000 of retirement income. However, it is often much harder to do that near or during retirement. Again, the earlier one begins planning, the more potential we have.

There are only three kinds of investments that offer tax-free characteristics: ROTH IRA's, muni-bonds and cash-value life insurance. Few people I meet with have very much in their tax-free bucket before they work with me. If it's too late for you to do something like this, you can help your adult children

For many people, the **tax-deferred bucket** is the next best thing. You "postpone" paying the tax. Tax-deferred buckets are traditional IRA's, 401(k)'s, 403(b)'s, and other "qualified" accounts as well as annuities. When you hold money in tax-deferred investments you have much more control of when you get taxed (upon taking withdrawals).

Unlike non-qualified annuities (non-IRA type money), qualified money such as traditional IRA's have to be slowly withdrawn (and fully taxed) at age 70½. These forced withdrawals (whether the market is up big or crashing) are called Required Minimum Distributions (RMDs).

For many of my clients who do not need to take the mandatory RMD's to maintain their desired lifestyle, this is a big thorn in their side and can sometimes even push them into a higher tax-bracket. These folks hate RMDs.

Taxable investments are those in which you get a 1099, K-1 or a similar tax form every year which notifies the I.R.S. that you earned interest, dividends, short or long term capital gains – whether you withdrew the gains… or not!

You must pay the taxes each year you have interest or gains. Even if your account balance is lower at the end of the year than it was at the beginning… the I.R.S. wants its share.

Most people that I see have the majority of their funds in the taxable and tax-deferred buckets and the least amount in the tax-free. Most folks quickly understand the benefits of making some smart money moves to reduce current taxes and increase spendable income. But like many things in life – timing is everything.

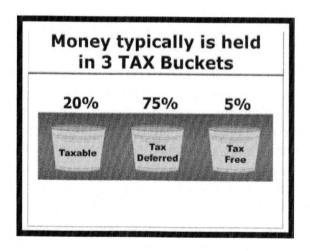

Do your three current tax buckets look more like the above or the ones depicted on the next page?

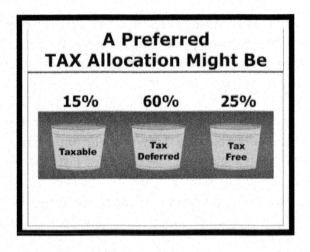

And as you read earlier, where you keep your money can affect how much of your Social Security checks get taxed... and sometimes at what tax rate. If you can reduce your taxes, you can spend more money and enjoy a better lifestyle on the same gross income. The two slides below show what I typically see in prospective client portfolios (top slide) and more like what I'd rather them have (bottom slide).

For most people there are simple money moves to get more of your funds in the best tax buckets for you and cut your tax bill. When you combine designing an investment portfolio and supplemental income stream by using the 3 buckets of risk along with wisely using the 3 tax buckets, you can truly transform your retirement years.

By properly employing all 6 buckets, you can dramatically slash your investment risk, enjoy more peace of mind and even cut your annual "contributions" to the I.R.S. Isn't money in your pocket better than in theirs? Making the "right" money moves is up to you. But it can make a real difference.

Basic Income Tax Calculations

In this next part of the book, I'm going to show you how a couple age 65 or older (who have done no special tax planning), can have up to $99,200 of taxable income and still be in the 15% marginal tax bracket. We will do this just using personal exemptions and standard deductions.

How did I get to this figure? First we take the top taxable income for a couple to remain in the 15% marginal tax bracket for 2017 is: $75,900. Then we add the $15,200 couples standard deduction (age 65+), plus and the $4,050 that each person gets as a personal exemption. The total of those figures is $99,200 of taxable income.

You may know that the most (under current law) that Social Security checks are taxable is 85% of the total Social Security income. So if a couple has $40,000 of Social Security income, then up to a maximum of 85% of that is subject to federal tax ($34,000). So at least $6,000 would be tax-free. How much of your Social Security income is subject to tax is based on a formula called "provision income".

Provisional income is the amount of your Adjusted Gross Income (AGI), plus half of your Social Security income, plus all tax-exempt interest (muni bonds).

One important thing to know about Provisional Income is that ROTH IRA distributions (which by the way do not have RMDs) and proper distributions from a well-designed life insurance policy do not count in the calculation. (Neither does income from a reverse mortgage).

Once you have that Provisional Income figure, you go to the chart below (which has not changed since 1994) and see how much of your Social Security income is subject to federal taxation.

So a couple with provisional income of under $32,000 would not have any of their Social Security income taxed by the IRS. But a couple with over $44,000 would have up to 85% of their Social Security checks subject to being taxed.

Taxation of Social Security benefits

Your Tax Filing Status	Provisional Income**	Amount of Social Security benefits that are subject to any taxation (I.R.S.)
Married filing jointly	Under $32,000	0%
	$32,000 - $44,000	Up to 50%
	Over $44,000	Up to 85%
Single, head of household, qualifying widow(er), married filing separately and living apart from spouse	Under $25,000	0%
	$25,000 - $34,000	Up to 50%
	Over $34,000	Up to 85%
Married - filing separately and living with spouse	Over $0	85%

**Provisional Income = AGI PLUS one-half of your SS benefit(s) PLUS all tax-exempt interest (muni bonds)

Anyway, forgetting Social Security taxation for the moment, how much federal income tax would this couple having $99,200 of taxable income pay to the IRS (per the above assumptions)? They would owe $10,453 to the IRS.

So yes much of their income was taxed at 15%, but a $10,377 total IRS tax bill on $99,200 of taxable income equals a total tax rate of about 10.46%, after taking in exemptions, standard deductions and some income ($23,300 in 2017) only being taxed at the 10.54% rate. That's called your "effective" tax rate.

The next tax bracket is taxed at a 25% rate. For married filing jointly, taxable income above $75,900 up to $153,100 is taxed at the marginal rate of 25%. I have a number of clients with a taxable income that we try and keep them from paying more taxes than at the 25% marginal tax rate, but have some others where RMD's etc. put then well into the higher brackets.

There are four more tax brackets above the 25% marginal tax (28%, 33%, 35% and 39.6%). Tax bracket levels for single filers are half of those for married filing jointly. And for modified adjusted taxable incomes (MAGI) of $200,000 for single filers and $250,000 for joint filers there is a 3.8% surtax on both ordinary income and even capital gains!

And of course there is the Alternative Minimum Tax that may apply for single filers with as little as $54,300 and joint filers with as little as $84,500 incomes in 2017. Another IRS GOTCHA!

How states (and municipalities) calculate their income tax is a whole different story and way beyond the scope of this book. Some states such as Florida and Texas have no state income taxes, others tax every dime of your income and do not tie it to your federal return. Some states, like California top out at about 13% state income tax rates. WOW! I think I would consider moving to a state with lower taxes. But I understand why the Californians love their state.

OK, so nobody reading that short section is going to be able to go out and charge folks to do their tax return, but I think it's important for you to come away with the knowledge of how Social Security is taxed as well as how much taxable income you can have and still pay an effective tax rate of under 11%.

A moment ago I promised a quick example of how I can help people (with some very basic and absolutely IRS approved techniques), pay as little as $2,000 in federal income taxes on $100,000 gross retirement income. That's $98,000/yr after tax!

Tom and Susan are 50 years old now and want to retire at age 65 at their same lifestyle that they enjoy today. They earn $100,000 now. They have $500,000 in their IRAs and Toms is contributing 10% of his income to a 401K plan at work with no company match at his new job. They also have about $120,000 in a taxable brokerage account. They estimate from their Social Security statements that they'll receive $70,000 in Social Security at age 65. They have no pensions but would like live in retirement... just like they do today. No lifestyle sacrifices!

They want to shift as much of their present and future savings into the tax-free bucket as they can. They now realize that if their IRAs grow at an average of 7% a year until they retire, the account will be worth some $1,379,000 then. They are worried about future RMDs and the effect on provisional income. They want to pay as little federal taxes on their Social Security income as possible. Truth be told, they want to pay as little total income tax as the law allows during their retirement.

They do not want to do a full ROTH conversion with the IRAs and pay over 25% income taxes on the conversion all at once but they'll have to do some ROTH conversions over time. They will also have to move the projected 7% average annual earnings on the IRAs (paying a bit of tax along the way) and putting the net proceeds ($24,500) into the tax-free bucket.

Those moves will keep the IRA value under at retirement $250,000 and their RMDs low enough to pay hardly any federal tax in retirement. They will also re-direct their after-tax net 401K contributions ($7,500) to the tax free bucket too.

Additionally, they are going to start moving about $7,000 a year from their taxable brokerage account (keeping $50,000 there as an emergency fund equaling 6 months of salary).

By just making those four financial moves, they are shifting about $53,000 (after-tax) a year from their tax-postponed and taxable buckets... into their tax-free bucket until retirement. They'll put themselves in the position of paying less than 2% on their retirement income (based on current tax laws). Where does this money go to qualify for the tax-free bucket?

Well, over half of it is going to fund their ROTHs (new $6,500 ones plus conversions). And the balance is going to fund a specially designed life insurance policy. Yup, life insurance. A description of how I use life insurance (like I do for myself) for the tax-free bucket is way beyond the scope of this book, but readers can contact me to learn more about this.

When they retire, the distributions from their ROTHS and life policies will not count against provisional income so their Social Security will not be taxed. The RMDs from their IRAs will be less than the standard deductions and personal exemptions so they will hardly be taxed either. In fact, in 2016 they would pay less than a $2,000 federal tax. Not too shabby.

Hate life insurance? I don't love it, but if we can use it and ROTHs to pay hardly any IRS income taxes during retirement, would that make sense to consider? Using just the ROTHs is not going to do the trick. Is your "not liking" life insurance going to cost you a fortune in paying future income taxes? Enough said.

We are now at the point where for most of the rest of this book, we'll be focusing on some retirement income planning strategies. With some retirement basics behind us, we're ready to GO!

Retirement Income Planning

I have to begin this section of the book by saying that each person's or couples retirement income goals are different. So is each person's tolerance for risk and longevity. There are many, many "un-knowables" over the next 20, 30 or 40 plus years – investment returns, tax rates, inflation rates, one's health care costs, etc. There are so many factors to be considered and even assumptions that have to be made.

There cannot be a cookie-cutter approach or perfect formula that you put some data in the "black box" and out pops a computerized income model that says where to invest, and which investments to tap and when to optimize a long and prosperous income plan.

When I do a retirement "income allocation" plan for a client, one that shows them how and where we are going to, year by year, fulfill their requested growing income (inflation until age 100 (longevity), I start with Social Security and/or guaranteed pensions on the left side of the spreadsheet.

Those guaranteed income streams that lasts until the person passes away (sometimes pensions have a survivor benefit but not usually 100% of the income) form the basic building block of the retirement income plan.

As you've probably gotten from my section on Social Security, in many cases, I prefer delaying filing for benefits to get the largest guaranteed monthly check possible. Of course, that may mean either working longer or taking income from other assets (IRA's, brokerage accounts, savings, etc.).

But for some people, this may not be the right strategy or even possible. However for many, this may be the best path, especially if one expects to live (or their spouse) a long life and wants as much guaranteed income with potential COLA's as possible – at least 15% of which is tax-free.

Then, in very simple terms, we just need to fill in the gap of that guaranteed income and the requested amount of growing income. We need to build the spreadsheet left to right.

This is where my job becomes both creative and fun, as except for the wealthy, there are many different directions someone could go to solve the lifetime income problem. Sometimes, one solution is clearly superior to other options. But I often use a combination of solutions best meet the plan.

In the pages that follow, I'll give you a few solutions that may provide you with the insight to plan your own retirement income. As I'm sure you can appreciate, no single solution for income is right for everyone. People have different income and legacy goals, life expectancies, risk tolerances and a number of other personal circumstances. Begin... with the end in mind.

The amount of retirement savings, real estate, life insurance, pensions, potential inheritances and the like all must play a critical role in determining the best course of action.

And of course, since the future is totally unpredictable, we must add that into the mix as well. So this is where the "safety-first" part of your total "income allocation" comes into play.

In essence, we want a large part of our "non-Social Security and pension income" to be guaranteed – at least enough to cover most, if not all of our basic retirement living expenses. If we have basic monthly retirement income expenses of $6,000, we want Social Security, pensions and some other guaranteed sources of income to provide most, if not all of that income. Perhaps a wise use of a reverse mortgage too.

And maybe we have discretionary income desires for another $15,000 a year for travel, hobbies, gifts, etc. then we can look to other assets and income sources and the "probability-based" mindset to provide for the "fun part" of retirement and legacy.

But if possible, most folks would rather "know" that their "monthly nut" (financial obligations) as one client of mine calls it is covered for as long as they live, with no market risk and no worries. No sleepless nights. Just peace of mind.

It's really uncanny, but this brings us back to the 3 buckets of risk and even the 3 tax buckets. I usually find that people that need guaranteed income (beyond Social Security and pensions) choose an amount that they want in their "Principal Protected" bucket... that pretty closely equals the amount of funds necessary to fill the "monthly nut" living expense requirement.

In other words, the amount of extra monthly income, above and beyond Social Security and any pensions, to handle most or all of their ongoing financial obligations can often be funded by the amount of their retirement savings they told me that they wanted in their Principal Protected bucket. Not always, certainly. Everyone's situation, needs and goals are different.

So what investments and/or products do I typically use for this "bucket" as part of the income allocation plan?

Well long ago, I had a number of my clients kept one or two years of this non-Social Security/pension income extra income in the bank: CDs and savings accounts. If the market was down, rather than selling stocks/mutual funds at low prices (sequence of return risk), we'd fund our income needs from the cash account. Having some cash on hand allowed our stocks to recover from a downswing - without selling stocks at low prices (and not having those shares available to eventually recover).

When the market recovers and raises, some of those gains are taken to replace the bank savings for the next potential market downturn. But with these FDIC investments, paying nearly no interest over the last 5-6 years, for most of my clients this is not a great option for this strategy. And as you know, CD's do not offer any lifetime income guarantees.

Although the principal is guaranteed with CDs, real inflation (the kind that you and I actually see in "real life", not what the government tells us it is) is running way higher than what the bank pays us in interest. To add insult to injury that interest is usually taxable -- whether we spend it or not. Paying taxes on puny CD interest income is a slap in the face to folks on a fixed income. But it's the law.

Many people do not realize this, but there is a sequence of "interest rate" risk with CDs and savings accounts. Just like the last half a dozen years, there will be period of extremely low interest rates again sometime in the future.

I worked with one CPA who told me that many of his elderly clients who lived on "safe" CD interest only (when rates were 3%-6% in the mid 2000's) were now having to deplete principal in order to make ends meet. The same thing could be said for those who are re-investing in bonds at much lower interest rates than they enjoyed before.

So yes, your principal is safe with these bank FDIC savings vehicles, but when inflation outpaces your after-tax earned interest, your purchasing power decreases. Your bank account statement does not show a decrease in value, but when you go to spend those assets when inflation is higher than your net after-tax interest earned, you have a loss of buying power. You need more dollars to buy the same amount of "stuff".

And of course, CD's do not give you any protection from longevity risk either. But many annuities do including fixed indexed annuities with an income rider. Let's look at what many of my clients decide to use for most of their "Protected Principal" risk bucket and exactly why they often choose it.

Fixed Indexed Annuities

You've probably seen the TV and magazine ads from the guy who "hates annuities… and thinks you should too". He owns one of the biggest investment advisory firms in the country and is worth $3.7 BILLION (Forbes). Like me, he is a fiduciary.

His newest commercials say that he "would rather die and go to hell than sell an annuity" and "I'll never sell an annuity". He's mostly talking about very high-cost variable annuities sold by many stockbrokers. I wouldn't sell one of those now either!

He and his multi-millionaire clients don't need annuities to make their "monthly nut". He could lose 90% of his assets in the stock market and still be very wealthy. With his wealth, he doesn't have longevity risk either. He could live to be age 650 and never run out of money. He's very different from you and I.

There is one other reason why he hates annuities. He doesn't get paid on them. His fee-only firm charges his clients a fee based on the amount of money his firm manages for the client. It's a fee for "assets under management" arrangement. In fact, he makes so much profit in quarterly fees, he'll even pay any surrender charges or early withdrawal penalties one may have in an annuity they own -- if they move those funds to his firm. Hmmm… maybe this partly explains how he is a billionaire!

There's nothing wrong with fees in and of itself. In fact, I and thousands of other investment advisors reps across the country charge fees for assets under management as well. It's the fastest growing way to be compensated in the financial world (as opposed to being paid trading commissions like the old days). Even the US government prefers fees over commissions, despite fees being more expensive for clients over time.

In my personal practice, my clients pay our firm investment management fees for assets that we manage for them in the low and moderate risk buckets percentages they want.

But what about the Principal Protected bucket? Since he is a fiduciary like I am, and must put his client's interests before his own, I have lot of important questions for him: "Where are you going to put your client's money that is protected from market risk and can earn respectable returns"? "What investments are you going to tell your non-multimillionaire clients (minimum investment with him is $500,000 according to his ads) to place money that they cannot afford to lose?" "What investments do you offer to take sequence of returns risk off of the table?" "Which of your investments totally eliminate longevity risk?"

In my mind, an advisor cannot truly be a fiduciary and have 100% of the clients best interest at heart, if one advises every single person that all annuities have no place in any income portfolio. In fact, the best academic research clearly shows that blanket statement is false. He's just a glorified pitchman.

As you'll see in a moment, certain annuities (fixed indexed and SPIAs) can do some things that no other investment can do both of – take away longevity and sequence of returns risk.

Before I continue, let me write a few words about financial products and services. ALL financial products are just tools. Each financial product: stocks, bonds, mutual funds, ETF's, limited partnerships, real estate, SPIAs, fixed annuities, reverse mortgages, CDs, etc., have a specific purpose just like tools do.

You use a screwdriver to screw two materials together. You do not use it to put a nail in the wall. A saw is great tool to cut a piece of wood, but it makes an awful wrench. You get the idea. Each type of financial product has a unique function. Each product has pros... and cons. When used properly it will do the job well. When used inappropriately – you've got a problem.

The same can be said about fixed indexed annuities (FIA) or a SPIA (explained later). Most are best suited to provide a contractual guaranteed lifetime (single or joint) income without stock market risk. An FIA is <u>not</u> meant to compete with the high potential returns of real estate, stocks, ETFs or equity mutual funds (when any of these does what you hope it will).

In these economic times of extremely low interest rates, a FIA can offer competitive returns to CD's and bonds with the added guarantee of providing an income you cannot outlive.

It is important to note that any contractual "guarantee" issued by an insurance company is solely backed by the financial strength and the "claims paying ability" of the insurer. Throughout this book, when I refer to guarantees of a FIA, I am referring to the contractual guarantee as described above.

Having written that regulatory disclaimer, I almost always recommend insurers with very high financial ratings (AM Best etc.) that have an unbroken history of making good on their promises (contractual guarantees) for many decades.

Insurance companies are very different from banks in that they have stricter "reserve" requirements. In fact, ten major US banks have over $60 BILLION dollars of their Federal Reserve

"Tier 1 capital reserves" requirements invested in life insurance policies backed by the "claims paying ability" of life insurers.

This asset class is good enough to satisfy the tough Federal Reserve with regards to being "Principal Protected" enough to be called Tier 1 capital, that so many banks own a lot of it. So shouldn't it be worthy of consideration for individuals?

All annuity income guarantees (including SPIAs) operate from the basis of math and actuarial science. It's actuarial science that academic researchers refer to as "mortality credits". And no type of investment, other than insurance, can provide mortality credits. It's the mathematical science of risk-pooling.

If you own life insurance, you already have mortality credits working on your behalf. How else can a life insurance company pay $1,000,000 death benefit on a 27 year old male who had only made one $35 monthly premium and then gets killed by a drunk driver? The insurer knows that most 27 year olds will live for many decades and prices this into the required premiums.

Actuarial science allows the insurance company to pay that death benefit because they know exactly how many 27 year old males will die in any given year. They don't know which ones will die, but they know how many will. That's actuarial science.

On the opposite side of that science is how long 91 year old females will live and be paid a continuing income from an annuity. They don't know which ones will pass away, but they know how many will each year going forward. It's just science.

By leveraging mortality credits, income annuities can provide amazing "retirement income alpha". Only insurance companies can manufacture high cash-flow that is totally uncorrelated to the volatile markets and perfectly hedges the risk of living too long. You cannot get valuable mortality credits anywhere else.

Insurance companies work both sides of the coin (actuarial science) to their benefit. The risk to the insurer of a life insurance policy is the policyholder dying too soon. The risk to the insurer of an annuity is someone living way too long.

Whether it is life insurance premiums or annuities guaranteed income, the insurance company pools 10,000's of lives to reduce their risk and offer the lowest life insurance premiums and highest annuity income payouts possible.

Here's something to think about. Many folks ask me, what is the internal rate of return on a guaranteed income annuity? I answer them by saying, "what do you want it to be?" The truth is, the insurance company does NOT set that rate of return.

You see, YOU (and perhaps your spouse) determine what the true internal rate of return will be – by how long one or both of you will live. That's mortality credits providing guaranteed retirement income alpha that you cannot get anywhere else.

Mortality credits are based on a person's age and gender. If you and/or your spouse are very healthy, the likelihood is that one/both of you will live longer than the average person's life expectancy. To get an even better return – just live longer!

There is one more advantage of income annuities (and SPIAs) that is similar to Social Security and pensions and addresses a potential retirement risk – deflation. Deflation is the opposite of inflation where prices (and most asset values) go down.

In the event that the U.S. ever goes through a period of deflation (which the Federal Reserve fears more than inflation), annuity income, like Social Security and pension income will be worth even more as those monthly paychecks would remain the same, while your costs of living would reduce. Deflation is a risk that the "probability-based" folks will always have, while the "safety-first" folks can avoid much of deflation risk.

Before we get back to planning a growing retirement income for the next 30 plus years and how fixed indexed annuities (and mortality credits), let me give you a general example of how an FIA might play a major role to improve a "safety-first" plan.

This example will show how $600,000 invested in an FIA now can most likely equal the heavy "income" lifting of $1,785,000 by using actuarial science and mortality credits. You see in the "Probability-based" mindset using "asset allocation", one needs 100% of their money invested at all times in order to make the withdrawal rate (4%, 2.8% or 2%) work with a 90% probability.

Nelson and Sandra are both 56 years old. They have just over $1,000,000 saved now, most of which is in an old 401(k) that he rolled over into an IRA. They'd like to retire at age 66 (which is their full retirement age with Social Security) and have $50,000 of income on top of what they'll get from Social Security in order to meet their anticipated monthly expenses (safety-first).

They feel comfortable with the withdrawal rate of 2.8% that Morningstar suggests. If that's the case, their million dollars in savings will have to grow by 6% per year to reach $1,785,000. That future goal figure would give them an initial investment income of $50,000 a year growing by inflation at the 2.8% withdrawal rate. Could another 2008 derail this plan? Yup.

Are you with me? Excluding any additional savings for their retirement, if their current dollars "can" grow at 6% a year (remember that they are getting close to the Retirement Red Zone so they won't be overly aggressive), their savings will have grown to the number which at a 2.8% withdrawal rate will give them a starting income of $50,000 when they retire at age 66 to supplement their Social Security to meet basic expenses.

However, since their funds are all invested in the market now, they have sequence of returns risk that could either work for them... or against them. They want to have confidence in their future retirement and would like as much predictability as possible. David Gaylor says that "sequence of returns risk is the biggest gamble pre-retirees and retirees alike will make".

So how can $600,000 invested in an FIA do the heavy income lifting to equal a portfolio fully invested in the market, and likely do so with much less market risk? No market losses ever.

Well $600,000 is the amount needed to (based on the index's performance of one of my favorite FIA's over the last 12 years) to cover the full $50,000 income goal from savings ten years from now. To be clear, that $50,000 income figure is not guaranteed, but if the next ten years look anything like the last 10-12 years, we should be right in that ballpark. FYI: only $32,000 is guaranteed if the FIA earns absolutely NO returns during the first 10 years – but that has never happened before and that would be the least of their financial problems if it ever did happen. I'll explain exactly how FIAs work in a moment.

So we used 60% of their million dollars in savings to go into the FIA which on its own should be able to give them most or all of their extra monthly income needed for their basic living expenses in retirement. The other $400,000 can be left to grow without too much worry about sequence of return risk.

Coincidently, their 3 buckets of risk was originally 65% in the Principal Protected bucket, 10% in the Low Risk bucket and 25% in the Moderate Risk bucket. With such a big percentage invested with no market risk, they can now afford to take more risks in the other two buckets. Based on their new retirement income plan (we're just getting started with lots more options to really optimize their retirement), they have modified their 3 risk buckets to 60%/15%/25% respectively.

The $400,000 leftover would be split between the two other risk buckets. These funds would grow to $786,000 over the next ten years (at an assumed 6% average rate).

Unlike the "Probability-based" mindset where they would need to have 100% of their money to generate the $50,000 (at a 2.8% withdrawal rate), they'll likely have nearly $800,000 extra cash to buy a boat, travel the world, leave a legacy, etc. However, if nothing like that interested them and they used the same 2.8% withdrawal rule on these additional funds, we just increased their retirement lifestyle by about $22,000 a year.

So not only did employing an FIA with a portion of their savings take sequence of returns risk off the table for their future "monthly nut", it gives them a huge amount of extra money to do all kinds of things in retirement with the rest... or add some $22,000/year to their lifestyle. That's a 44% increase to their income from savings due to actuarial science and math.

Your "numbers" will be different. But that is how Nelson's and Sandra's $600,000 today can do the work of $1,785,000 tomorrow. Are you now willing to learn more about FIA's?

Let me give a general description of how FIA's work and avoid stock market risk. As the name fixed indexed annuity implies, the interest "return" is determined by an index or indexes such as the S&P 500, Dow or the Barclays Bond index.

Once you pay your annuity premium to the insurance company, the company invests those funds into their general account which is heavily invested in bonds that pay interest.

The insurer could pay you an interest rate like a CD from what it earns on its own bond investments minus their overhead, expenses and profit margin. Your bank does something very similar, in that it pays the depositor an interest rate that depends on its loan portfolio interest income minus its overheard, expenses and profit margin.

As I edit this section many FIAs will offer their policyholders a fixed one year rate of 1.75% or so (fixed account) right now. Better than most banks, but not very appealing to most folks.

As the owner of an FIA, you have the right to forego getting that fixed interest rate and have those interest payments buy options on an index(es) such as the S&P 500, NASDAQ, etc.

By using options, you can participate in the upside of the index when it goes up. But there is a catch – you don't get all or even most of the upside in a good year. Because of the option strategy(s) you choose, you are "limited" in the amount of interest that can be credited to your annuity by a "cap", "spread" or a certain "participation" rate. I'll get to these terms in a moment.

Also by using options instead of investing your actual principal, you can never get a loss since your funds were never invested in the index. And the worst thing that can happen with the option strategies the insurer uses, is that the options expire worthless. When that happens, no interest is credited to your policy that year. In other words, you get a zero return.

When the indexes crash like in 2000, 2001, 2002 and 2008, ZERO is your hero! It's much better to get NO return... than to experience a big loss. Your principal can never go backwards due to losses in an index. No sequence of return risk at all.

And when the index goes up, because of the use of options, your gain is limited by a cap, spread or a participation rate. A "cap" is the <u>most</u> the interest will credit one year (say 4.25%), based on the index used, the cost of the options and the amount the insurance company can spend on the options (which is about equal to the interest they would have paid you in the fixed account).

A "participation rate" means that you would get a certain percentage of the index's gain such as 55%. A participation rate can give you the potential for more upside in a BIG year.

So with a participation rate of 55% and if the index went up by 6%, your policy would be credited with an interest rate of 3.3% that year. When the index does 11.2% with a 55% spread, your interest credit would be 6.105%. Again, you never participate in any index losses, so zero is always your hero.

Like participation rates, a "spread" also allows for some more potential gains when the index has big gains. By "spread" the insurer uses that spread percentage to buy more options. A 2.75% spread means that you don't get any interest credited unless the index beats that amount (the spread).

You get ALL of the gain above that amount credited to your policy. For example, if the index does 7.75% with a 2.75% spread, your account would be credited with 5% interest. If the index returned 14% then you would get credited 11.25%. If the index only did 2%, the spread is larger than the gain and you would get no interest that year.

There are another two attractive features of the FIA which you should know about that sets it apart from most every other type of investment.

The "annual lock-in" feature says that once interest is credited to your account, it becomes principal and at that point is never subject to market losses. Those gains become part of your protected account value. In most cases, on every policy anniversary, any interest gained is credited to your account automatically and becomes principal.

The only way to lock-in gains of stocks, bonds, mutual funds, real estate, etc. is to sell the asset. Of course, unless the asset is inside an IRA or similar IRS qualified account, there will be a tax due on the gain. In any annuity, there is no tax due until money is withdrawn. This is an important advantage if you are using investments from your taxable risk bucket to fund your FIA prior to retiring and waiting to take your lifetime income. You won't get a 1099 tax form nor owe a tax until taking income.

The other nice feature is the "annual reset". This means that the beginning value(s) of the index or indexes you choose to allocate your funds in each policy year, resets on your annual policy anniversary. This is a valuable feature.

How is this important? Let's go back to October 16, 2007 and say you retired and rolled over your 401(k) to buy a $400,000 FIA and had 100% of your index allocated to the S&P 500 index when the S&P 500 index closed at 1538 that day. A year later, on October 16, 2008 (your 1st policy anniversary) the S&P index closed at 946… a -38% loss. Talk about sequence of return risk!

As you know, because your principal was never invested in the market, your $400,000 did not lose a dime. Zero was your hero. But this is where annual reset comes into play. For your next policy year, the index resets to where it ended the year before – at 946. Now all of next year's interest which will be credited to you policy is calculated from that index value to where the index closes a year later – not on the original index of 1538 when you bought the annuity.

On October 16, 2009 the S&P 500 index closed at 1087. That is a 14.9% gain (subject to caps, spreads or participation rates) and would be the basis of your interest credited to your policy that year. And now for the next policy year, 1087 would reset to be the starting index value. This is very powerful – especially when waiting to take retirement income.

It doesn't work that way with stocks or mutual funds. If you retired and rolled over your 401(k) and bought $400,000 of the Vanguard S&P 500 mutual fund on October 16, 2007, there is annual no lock-in nor annual reset. Your mutual fund would have lost the full -38% that the index did in the first year you owned it. Your mutual fund lost a whopping $152,000.

And you would need a 61% gain in the index to just get you back to breakeven (from a 38% loss). With most investments your principal is never protected and your past gains are never locked in either. FIAs protect your principal during a market crash and can perform pretty well during recovery periods.

In fact, five years after you bought that mutual fund, the S&P 500 had still <u>not</u> reached where you originally invested. On October 16, 2012, the index closed at 1455 (still below 2008).

The annual lock-in and reset features can certainly offset some of the disadvantages of not getting the full market gains in big up years due to caps, spreads and participation rates.

All FIAs offer the potential for respectable gains when the index(es) do well, but protect you from all losses and sequence of returns risk when the markets go down. Again, for most people, the FIA is attractive for the guaranteed lifetime income aspect, rather than for attempting to get stellar returns.

In addition to many indexes used, caps, spreads and participation rates, there are "time periods" that are used to measure potential returns and interest credited.

As just discussed, annual point to point calculates the index return from the day your policy gets issued (your effective date) to a year later (your policy anniversary) and does so year after year. The index value at the start of the policy year is compared to one year later (subject to caps etc.). Some policies only count index gains (lock-in and reset too) every two or even three years in order to determine your interest earned. There is also monthly averaging, monthly sum and daily averaging indexing calculations. I'm sure there are other methods too.

There are literally hundreds of FIAs available for sale from dozens and dozens of insurers. Most of them have more than one index available and more than one of the indexing strategies described above. For the layman, it can be very confusing at first. But again, the main purpose is usually to get a guaranteed lifetime income stream.

The biggest questions I am asked is what index and/or strategy is best? Is it spreads, caps or participation rates with annual point to point, monthly sums, etc.?

In my opinion, there is no right answer. It all depends on what the client thinks the index(es) might do the next year. If we are expecting a big year with really good returns, we might opt for a spread or participation rate. But if we are expecting the market to go down, then putting the funds in the fixed interest account may be the best thing (assuming we are right).

In most FIAs, you can diversify you index allocations to different indexes with different caps, spreads, etc. and can even place a portion of the funds in the fixed account.

But this is a long term investment. Forgetting about the years prior to retirement (as you'll see the earlier you get started the better), we're talking about filling a potential two to three decade or more guaranteed retirement income need.

Our financial goal is to create another predictable and sustainable income stream that has a contractual guarantee for either a single lifetime or a joint lifetime through the use of a fixed index annuity.

And on top of that, for most of my clients, I want to build the potential for annual income increases to help address inflation risk as best we can. My favorite FIAs do a good job of that but like everything in this world... there are pros and cons to each.

We are looking to add to our guaranteed Social Security and any pension checks to form a large percentage of our monthly income needs. Our monthly "nut" as my client says.

In my own planning practice, I choose from 3 or 4 FIAs highly-rated insurers (AM Best, etc.) that I understand very well and that have features and benefits that I believe will be best for my clients over the long run. Again, for most FIAs, this financial "tool" is positioned for income that can last as long as you do – without regard to returns once the guaranteed income begins.

Now in addition to not getting the full market gains (however you will never get a market loss) there are two main objections to adding an FIA to your retirement income plan.

We just discussed spreads, caps and participation rates. Every year, these are subject to change a bit. Not usually by a lot but they can and do move up and down. The biggest reason for this is the interest rates that the insurer is earning on their own portfolio (their general account) and the cost of options.

These "moving parts" are not too much different than an insurer deciding what dividend to pay their policyholders on whole life insurance contracts. The dividend is based on a number of factors, including changes in interest rates, claims paid and company expenses. I've seen caps, spread and participation rates go up and down by a bit throughout the year as my clients have their policy anniversaries and we get their annual statements.

In many policies, these changes have absolutely no bearing on guaranteed income once the policy owner decides to "turn-on" their guaranteed lifetime income stream. Once it's guaranteed, its guaranteed – no matter what changes may be made on caps, etc. That's an important distinction to know.

The other objection that comes up is liquidity. Most FIAs have a declining surrender charge during the first 10 years or so. Since the insurer is making long term promises to the policyholder, they need to commit their capital (your premium) to long term investments and planning. Having that capital for a longer time enables the insurer to give the client better income guarantees or other benefits. An early redemption of funds would derail those plans.

Surrender charges are meant to protect the insurer if a policyholder decides to cash-out early. Surrender charges typically start at a 10% "penalty" in the first year and slowly decline to no penalty or no charge in the last year of the surrender period (9-12 years). Once the surrender charge period is over the owner is free to cash-out at any time.

Most every FIA has a no-penalty "free withdrawal" amount during the surrender period in which the policyholder can take out 5%-10% of their initial premium without any penalty. This covers most of my client's needs and is sometimes even part of the retirement income plan that I design for them.

Let's say you bought a $200,000 FIA with a 10% initial surrender charge and a 10% free withdrawal provision. If you are in the second year of your contract and want to take out $28,000 for any reason, and the surrender charge declined to 9%, you would only pay that charge on the withdrawal over the $20,000 allowed amount. In this case, $720 ($8,000 x 9%).

Most FIA's have no surrender charges for death or someone that needs to go to a nursing home. And I always make sure my clients have funds invested elsewhere, in case of most any other kind of emergency. In any case, a 10% maximum surrender charge is much less costly to a retiree than having to sell stocks in a 20%, 35% or 50% market crash.

I mentioned earlier that an FIA may play an important role in a retirement income... unless you are wealthy and have a large amount of assets in non-IRA and non-401(k) type funds (the taxable bucket). I would still consider an FIA for 401(K) rollovers since there are few other sources of guaranteed lifetime income and the taxation is the same in any type of qualified account – no matter where it is invested.

For purposes here, I define wealthy as those with at least $5 million in assets exclusive of their primary residence. For most of these people, rather than an FIA, I look at an indexed life insurance (IUL) policy - if a guaranteed income stream is not important to them. Why life insurance and a specifically an IUL?

In an IUL the caps, spreads and participations rates are 2-3 times better than most FIAs so an IUL offers much more upside - with the same downside protection of... "zero is your hero". Just like any annuity, gains inside of the IUL contract are tax-deferred. But unlike an FIA (unless it is a ROTH IRA), the death benefit is always tax-free to the heirs.

And depending upon how the life policy is structured, we can get access to the cash value in the policy without triggering any income taxation – including supplemental retirement income. Tax-free access to the cash value and supplemental income distributions can be very, very attractive.

I have many non-wealthy clients that use an IUL for their retirement plan. If they can fund their IUL over 4-7 years and are not planning on touching funds in their IUL contract for 10 years or so, this is a great ROTH IRA alternative (tax-free).

In fact, I personally own five IUL contracts right now and they are 100% of my personal retirement plan. However, I would never advise anyone else have 100% in ANY financial strategy.

Or, many of my clients have old whole life or another type of universal life insurance policies that are not built to provide a tax-free supplemental retirement income stream. Many of these folks will do what's called a 1035 tax-free exchange to their new IUL. That is the IRS code that allows a non-taxable transfer of cash value from one insurance contract to another.

The first book that I wrote back in 2013, was written for folks like me, that the IRS says we make too much money to contribute to a ROTH IRA. And even if that wasn't the case, the maximum contribution of $6,500 a year would not give me the retirement lifestyle I'm looking for. But a properly structured and funded IUL can do a great job.

Similarly, my second book was written for folks who were

looking for a fixed annuity accumulation or CD alternative and like the benefits of an IUL: 1) of potential double-digit gains when the market does well and protection when the market crashes, 2) tax-deferral and 3) tax-free death benefit with 4) some potential long-term care benefits to boot.

By the way, I might add here that for those folks who were sold a variable annuity or have a fixed annuity that does not offer an attractive guaranteed income, a 1035 tax-free exchange can be done to a new, state-of-the-art FIA as well.

Just like everything else in this world, no investment product is perfect. That includes every FIA and IUL. Each and every investment option that exists... has its own pros and cons.

Single Premium Immediate Annuities (SPIA)

There is another financial tool that has a long history and substantial academic research as another potential solution to creating a guaranteed lifetime income stream (again based on the financial strength and claims paying ability of the insurer). Way back in 1965, Professor Menahem Yaari wrote about the value of a SPIA and its potential role in retirement planning.

In fact, do you remember the Wall Street Journal article entitled "Say Goodbye to The 2% Rule"? Here's a quote from Dr. Wade Pfau as part of a solution to deal with their 2% rule: "Use annuities instead of bonds. Pairing the most plain-vanilla type of annuity—called a single-premium immediate annuity—with stocks, retirees can generate income more safely and reliably than if they use bonds for that piece of their portfolio". He went on to say: "There is no need for retirees to hold bonds.

Instead, annuities, with their promise of income for life, act like super bonds with no maturity dates."

Replacing the bond portion of a portfolio with a SPIA (or a FIA) is a smart idea if you agree interest rates will continue to rise. I usually prefer FIAs over SPIAs and I'll explain why in a moment, but this is a very important concept where you can shift both credit risk and the risk of increasing interest rates from your pocket to an insurance company. They have actuarial science and use mortality credits for their protection.

In its most basic form, a SPIA is a financial product issued by an insurance company that in return for a single lump-sum premium, the insurance company promises to pay a guaranteed monthly income for your life.

The larger the premium the higher the guaranteed income. The income payment is based on your age and sex (women live longer), current interest rates and is based on life expectancies as determined by the insurer. For non-qualified funds (non-IRA), a SPIA can be much more tax-efficient than an FIA.

Payment quotes can change daily (with interest rates) but a 65 year old male with a lump sum premium of $300,000 would be guaranteed a single life income stream of 6.25% (as I write this today) or $18,750 per year for the rest of his life.

If he lives to age 102, he'll get $693,750 in total income from this annuity over his lifetime. If he dies in 4 years, he'll only get $75,000. That's all, since it is based on his lifetime only. If he died too early, he's out of luck. Again in its most basic form, there is no refund and no death benefit. No cash value at all.

It's not very different than Social Security. Most people pay their FICA tax for decades to get a Social Security check at retirement. Excluding any potential spousal benefits, if they die before the file for benefits, they will get nothing in return. If they die a few years after they start getting benefits, that's all they get. If they live to 102, those checks keep rolling in, month after month (with some COLAs along the way).

And it's the exact opposite with life insurance. If you make 1 monthly life insurance premium and then die, the insurance company is going to pay a huge death benefit (in relation to the size of the premium paid). The insurer got killed on that policy.

Contrarily, if you pay premiums for 60 years and then die, the life insurance company did pretty well. All insurance works the same way (using the law of large numbers) and has served mankind well for centuries.

Like Social Security, the people that die early, effectively pay the benefits for the people that live a long life. Again, it's called "mortality credits". This totally removes your longevity risk. Dr. Yaari called annuities an "optimal" retirement solution.

There are SPIAs that pay a reduced payout amount on two lives, or offer a refund if you didn't get enough income to refund your initial premium, or have a 10 or 20 year minimum payment period regardless of death. Some SPIAs offer COLAs so your income can increase over time, but all of these products have much lower initial guaranteed income payouts.

And quite frankly, an FIA works on the same basic concept of mortality credits with its guaranteed lifetime income provisions. Although there is typically a cash value and/or death benefit until your early-mid 80's so you have much more control and access to your savings than you would with a SPIA.

With an FIA, the income continues even after there is no cash left in the policy. You bought it for guaranteed income and you'll get that. But with the FIA, for some 15-25 years or so, you'll also have a death benefit for heirs if you die, and have access to any cash in the policy if that becomes more important than many more years of income at some point.

And in many states, some FIAs offer some additional potential benefits if you need long-term care (LTC) in a licensed facility. Because there is usually no cost for this potential benefit, you may not ever get anything extra at all.

NEVER buy an income FIA for some potential LTC benefits. It does not replace a traditional long term care insurance policy as it may never pay an additional benefit at all. Each FIA has its own terms and conditions and if you understand them, you'll know why there is no cost to this LTC benefit in most cases.

Generally, a SPIA will give you a higher guaranteed income stream than a FIA. But with an FIA you have much more flexibility and you can even move your money elsewhere (subject to any surrender charges) at any time you'd like.

For most of my clients, when they compare a SPIA with a FIA, the FIA wins most of the time when all the pros and cons are taken into consideration. Although some of my clients do use a SPIA for a portion of their retirement plan.

Sometimes we use a SPIA to provide an income for a short

period of time (5-10 years) while the Social Security income will rise by delaying their filing. In this case, we use a SPIA with a 5 or 10 year "period certain". The SPIA makes a payment for only that number of years and is done. Of course, it is a much higher payment than a lifetime payout.

Or perhaps we use a SPIA for a portion of the planned income to get a higher guaranteed income than a FIA – despite the typical lack of access to your capital and/or death benefit.

Three Sample Income Allocation Plans

OK, so moving left to right on the retirement income plan spreadsheet we started with Social Security income on the far left and any guaranteed pension income next to that.

The next column or columns would typically be guaranteed income from a FIA or perhaps a SPIA. But this is where some financial creativity can play a huge role as you'll see in the paragraphs that follow. This is the fun part – designing income!

As I've mentioned earlier, income allocation creates as much of a predictable and sustainable retirement income stream that pays for all or most of our monthly expenses as possible. We want to remove as much longevity risk and sequence of returns risk as possible with this side of the spreadsheet. Again, Income Allocation leans heavily to the "safety-first" mindset.

For most middle and upper class Americans, retirement is all about cash-flow. Using Social Security, pensions and perhaps an FIA that has a contractual guarantee for either a single lifetime or a joint lifetime forms that basic building block of cash-flow.

And if that FIA offers the potential for annual income increases (like Social Security) to help address inflation risk, that's even better. Most do not.

Now before we look at an example, I must reiterate that each and every person or couple is unique. They each have different amounts and types of financial assets, income needs and/or goals, likely longevities, risk tolerances, potential Social Security income and filing strategies, pension incomes, and potential inheritances and so on.

But just for fun, let's look at Jim and Mary. He is 66 and she is 65 and both are in good health and expect to live a long life. They told me to plan on at least one of them living to age 100.

That is a lot of years of being "unemployed" as well as many years they face sequence of returns risk, inflation risk, deflation risk, tax increase risk, and rising health care costs.

They have accumulated about $830,000 in savings – all in a 401(k) and IRAs. Jim also had about $17,800 cash value in a small paid-up whole life policy with a $26,000 death benefit.

Their home is not paid for, but they are not sure if or when they might move or downsize. So we left the house out any planning. They also have some $15,000 - $20,000 in their checkbook and bank accounts which I left out of the plan too.

Jim plans on working until age 70 when he will file for Social Security benefits. Not only does he want to collect the maximum monthly check that he can, should Mary outlive him, he wants her to get the biggest survivor check possible for as long as she lives. Mary told me that this was an "act of love".

Mary has not earned much Social Security benefits on her own earnings record since she spent most of her career working on three raising children, etc. She will file for spousal benefits once she turns Full Retirement Age.

In today's dollars they would like a net after-tax (money they can spend) of $75,000 beginning at his retirement at age 70, which at 3% inflation will be $84,400 in four years. Look how much that desired income grew in just 4 years at 3%!

In trying to meet inflation risk, they asked me to give them a "pay raise" of 3% a year for the rest of their lives. Social Security COLAs helped me a bit in this regard, but I only assumed average Social Security COLAs of 2%.

Fourteen years from now at age 80, they will need $113,400 of after-tax income to buy what $75,000 does today at 3% inflation. At age 90, they will need $152,450 a year – after paying taxes to keep up with inflation at 3%. At age 95, they will need $176,742. Few people anticipate the real damage that inflation can do to someone on a "fixed income".

When I asked them about how they would like their savings distributed between the 3 buckets of risk, they told me that they wanted it all in the Principal Protected bucket. They had had enough of the buy, hold... and pray asset allocation portfolios. This told me they were 100% in the "safety-first" mindset.

Although I understand where they are coming from, with such low interest rates for the last five years and conceivably for the next 3-5 years at least, that is not prudent.

So for the $830,000, they settled on 70% in the Principal Protected bucket... and 30% split between the other two buckets with a larger focus on limiting drawdown, rather than returns.

All of that money will be subject to Required Minimum Distributions (RMDs) at age 70 ½ as well. So even someone who doesn't need the income from IRAs, will have to take it out and pay taxes on it. The IRS wants to finally get tax revenue from those tax-postponed plans (401k, 403b, traditional IRAs, SEPs, SIMPLE's, etc.). Don't get me started on that one!

Since all of their savings were in the tax-deferred bucket, we didn't spend much time on the 3 tax buckets conversation at that point. Looking at converting some of their IRAs to ROTHs (and paying taxes now) was not appealing to them so we left things as they are in this regard. But normally, I'd like to give some guidance there as well.

So how does income allocation work in this case (subject to their unique and individual personal financial preferences, etc.)? A plan based on certainty and not hope or speculation.

Even with today's income tax standard deduction and exemptions (which typically increase every year) they will be able to have gross income of about $100,000 and still be in the 15% marginal federal tax bracket. But we won't need $100,000 to net $84,400 (unless we live in San Francisco or N.Y. City).

Of course, not all of their Social Security will be subject to tax and depending on the state they live in there may be zero or 6% up to 13% of state and local income tax to pay. In this example we'll figure to pay a 12% total federal and state effective income tax rate. In this client example we'll need about $96,000 of gross income to net the desired $84,400 after tax income. Who knows what future tax rates will be?

Now let's build Jim and Mary's (of course these are not their real names) retirement income plan from left to right on the spreadsheet -- which I call their "retirement roadmap"!

If we are going to need about $96,000 of initial gross income once Jim turns age 70 and he files for Social Security benefits (at the maximum benefit he will ever get), income from both of their Social Security checks (Mary will wait one year) will be about $59,000 a year. I have this income projected to growing by 2.0% COLAs on average. This is 40% less than the historical 2.8% average Social Security COLA. I like to be conservative.

Under the old 4% withdrawal theory, they "could" take $33,200 out of their portfolio (adjusted to inflation each year) and add that to their Social Security income and their plan might work. It might. In fact, it might even leave a substantial legacy for their family. But the income could run dry 20 years into retirement too. It all depends on the sequence of returns.

Keep in mind that 60% of their income comes from Social Security and I only have that inflating by 2%, which means the other 40% of their income needs to generate returns that will combat inflation by more than 4% COLAs. Pretty unlikely.

And with Morningstar's recommended 2.8% withdrawal rate that you read about earlier in the book, that percentage equals an income of just $23,250 a year. Although that will take away some sequence of returns risk, it will not enable them to meet their desired income and lifestyle goals. That missing $10,000 (at 2.8% withdrawals) will cost them a lot of fun, travel and adventures during their retirement years.

With $59,000 coming from guaranteed monthly checks from Social Security, we only need 37,000 a year to complete their desired income. But that is more than even the 4% withdrawal rate that the Wall Street Journal denounced in their article "Say Goodbye to the 4% Rule" back in 2013.

As you recall, they wanted 70% in their Principal Protected bucket that is not subject to sequence of return risk. In this case, they invested $580,000 in one of my favorite FIAs. It's a favorite because, although they will get a lower initial guaranteed joint lifetime income, this particular FIA offers an option with attractive potential for increasing income.

Based on the past, the income is very likely to increase most years and do so at a rate of well over 3.5% on average. But for the spreadsheet projections, I only used 3%.

Now all FIAs will increase the guaranteed lifetime income based on delaying "turning on" that lifetime guaranteed income. So we're using that fact to our advantage and not turning on the guaranteed income until Jim turns age 77.

In the meantime, we'll take advantage of the no-surrender charge penalty-free withdrawals. We can take up to $58,000 a year after year one, without any penalty charge, but we don't need that much. We'll just take $27,500 from the FIA.

Without going year by year through the "retirement roadmap" (spreadsheet), I'll take the needed income by using free withdrawals until age 76 when he'll turn on their joint lifetime income. At that point, the income will be guaranteed for as long as either of them live – no matter what. Like Social Security, the COLAs are not guaranteed... but the income is.

And should they both die before the account is empty, their heirs will get any leftover funds that are in the policy. But because this FIA offers a guaranteed joint lifetime income, we eliminate all longevity risk for both of them.

Social Security checks eliminate longevity risk for a single person, but in a couple, once a spouse dies, the income goes from two monthly Social Security checks down to one check. The biggest check remains, but the smaller check disappears.

Getting back to Jim and Mary, you'll also recall that they were willing to spilt 30% of their savings into the other two risk buckets which equaled $250,000. Although I won't go into it here, rather than traditional "modern portfolio theory" they liked the tactical investment strategies of the 3rd party private wealth managers that my firm uses for the other two risk buckets. Again, they wanted to avoid big drawdowns.

These fee-only managers can go to cash when the market is trending downward. A few can even "short" the market and potentially profit when the markets go down. This willingness and ability to go to cash can reduce the "drawdown" (defined earlier) of the portfolio.

They invested the $250,000 in a diverse portfolio of our managers putting 65% into the low risk bucket managers and 35% with the moderate risk bucket managers.

With this size of investment, we can diversify funds going into the two other risk buckets and use 12-24 different private wealth managers who have different strategies and use different asset classes.

These wealth managers I have mentioned when combined in a portfolio sleeve (risk bucket) seek to achieve higher returns with less volatility over a full market cycle. They are poised to reduce volatility and some sequence of return risk versus a typical 60% equity and 40% bond portfolio.

In comparison to the Barclay's bond index and S&P 500, our low and moderate risk managers (as a group) have competitively performed along-side of the indices. Keep in mind that the goal of our managers has always been to have reduced volatility while being active in the market.

Although for the "plan" I'm only projecting 5% avg. annual returns, but the goal of the group of managers will be to handily out-perform that projection, with less volatility and smaller drawdowns than "buy and hold" along the way.

Back to Jim and Mary. In any case, because of their lifetime guaranteed income of the Social Security and the FIA, we only need a diversified portfolio of these managers to average a 5% annual return and simply take the IRS Required Minimum Distributions (RMDs) – about $9,500 at age 70.

There were no "aggressive" projected 8% annual returns (every year) that I often see in other advisor "plans". But to be frank, few advisors even give their clients a real income plan. Although for the "plan" I'm only projecting conservative returns and focuses on reducing sequence of returns risk.

The income allocation plan (with all of our conservative assumptions described above) meets their goal of increasing their initial after-tax income of $84,400 a year (about $7,000 a month) and grow that income by 3% annually to combat expected inflation. We also removed a tremendous amount of both sequence of returns risk and longevity risk too.

The guy "that hates annuities" is not going to give them a plan. He'll just give them every bit of the sequence of returns and longevity risk possible. That's not the kind of "retirement income plan" that Jim and Mary had any interest in.

There is only one problem with this plan. It's one that occurs in most all of the lifetime income roadmaps that I design for my clients. Virtually all plans, except for those folks who started out with a lot more money, started working with me 5-10 years before their retirement or had modest retirement income desires, had the same potential landmine. Death of one spouse.

The joint life expectancy of a couple Jim and Mary's age is 92. That means at least one of them is expected to live at least that long. But as discussed earlier the longer they both live, the longer their joint life expectancy will be extended.

In their plan, the problem arises at Mary's age 95, as I am assuming that Jim dies at age 94. At that time, Mary will "inherit" Jim's Social Security check and lose her own. Two monthly checks going down to one.

At that point, Mary's check would have been about $26,000 but she'll get Jim's check – not hers. So there will be an income shortfall at that point (or whenever either spouse passes).

So what to do we do about it? You will recall that they owned a home. By this time, it will have either been payed-off or they would have downsized (generating more available funds to invest). Although I'll write about reverse mortgages later on, this is another potential income fix too. Reverse mortgages give us many more potential planning opportunities.

I also mentioned that Jim had a paid-up whole life policy with a $26,000 death benefit. Since he was is very good health, we did a 1035 tax-free exchange to a new policy. If he only moved the cash value of $17,800 his new policy guaranteed death benefit would be $38,000. That's a 46% increase -- for just moving the cash value from one policy to another. Taking money from his left pocket and moving it to his right pocket.

But when discussing this, I suggested they consider adding just $100 a month premium to the new policy. By adding this small premium, the guaranteed death benefit would now be $83,000. That made complete sense to them – and especially Mary. So that's what they did.

Since the plan has Mary short about $26,000 when Jim dies, (guys usually go first), the death benefit will handle about three years of the income shortfall. So excluding any possibility of using the home, we took Mary to age 97 at the same income.

Before I go on, I should make clear that their retirement roadmap is a "living spreadsheet". We do not just "set it and forget it"! Each year we will refer back to the "plan" and make any adjustments necessary. Did they spend all of the money last year or need more? Did the investments do better or worse that year? Has anything else changed?

So what do you think about a plan like theirs? Would you like to see another client roadmap? Let's meet Tom and Connie (again, not their real names). Here's the short version.

Both are age 64 and would like to retire at age 66. Tom is not interested in discussing delaying his Social Security in order to get 8% delayed credits and leave a bigger Social Security check to Connie when he passes. About 14 months before meeting me, Connie had already started taking her Social Security.

Although they have amassed some considerable assets ($1.35 million) they had a modest retirement income goal of $65,000 after tax income (growing by 3% inflation). They had more interest in leaving a legacy (3 kids and to their church).

After working on their retirement income roadmap, I wanted to convince them to live a "larger retirement" lifestyle – at least for the first 10-15 years of their retirement. They earned it! They loved to travel. I didn't want them to have regrets in their later years that they missed out on seeing the world.

Many folks ask me to allow for more income in the early years of retirement when they are more active and reduce it at some point in their eighties. That makes sense, except for as they spend less on fun, they tend to spend more on health care (excluding any potential long term care needs).

At least I wanted to show them they did have the means to increase the initial desire of $65,000 to $80,000 after-tax income and leave a legacy. That's a 23% increase in lifestyle.

Using conservative assumptions in the plan, even if they

kept on enjoying that $80,000 inflation-protected income (never stop to "living it up" after 10-15 years) they'll still leave about $1,000,000 in legacy during their mid-eighties.

Again, starting from the left side of the spreadsheet, their combined Social Security is $52,000. As usual, I projected average annual COLAs of 2%.

When asked about the 3 buckets of risk, Tom wanted 25% in the Principal Protected bucket, but Connie wanted 55% there. They compromised on 40% for that bucket. So $550,000 would go into that bucket using an FIA.

Tom is an avid investor. He has always invested their money on his own and he didn't really want to pay for someone else to do that in retirement either.

But he and Connie understood that the distribution phase of retirement is very different than the accumulation phase. That's where sequence of return risk comes into play. And Connie would not let him forget that he, like most everyone, didn't do too well in 2008. "When's the next crash?" she said.

I suggested the wisdom in considering having our private wealth managers handle $300,000 of their savings since they had a past performance of lower drawdowns than his own personal investment track record. Plus, they both liked the idea of starting a relationship with a firm that could take over completely should Tom pass away before Connie.

For the FIA, they choose another one of my favorites. Unlike the annuity that Jim and Mary liked best, which had a much higher _guaranteed_ initial income, the one they chose had more potential for a higher initial income and one where the income would likely grow much faster too. They felt that at least one of them will live until their mid-nineties and wanted to make up for as much "lost income" as possible when they went from two Social Security check down to one (at the first death).

Although we could use the 10% free-withdrawal provisions of the FIA, we decided to not take any income it during the first nine years of retirement. We did not want to disturb the maximum potential of joint lifetime income. But at that point we projected an initial income stream of $50,000 from that annuity and that income growing by an about 3.5% each year.

Although in no way guaranteed to, this income should grow over time to about $90,000 a year at age 92 and continue to grow until they are both gone. Based on past performance that is a lower growth rate than what we might actually see.

Where does the retirement income come from until that time? In addition to their Social Security, I recommended that we spend down their taxable money first (unlike Jim and Mary they had about $190,000 in non-IRA brokerage accounts).

The rest was in their tax-postponed bucket (IRAs). Like many people, they had no money in the tax-free bucket. I hardly ever see more than $50,000 in the tax-free bucket.

Anyway, my firm would manage that $190,000 taxable bucket as well as $110,00 of their IRA funds ($300,000 total) since I was more confident in our managers ability to reduce sequence of return risk with their ability to go to cash rather than the traditional, buy and hold.

We would spend down the taxable account first and then the IRA we are managing. Essentially I was suggesting spending all of the money our firm managed first. When is the last time and you've heard of an investment advisor recommend that?

Tom would manage the rest of the funds himself. As far as the retirement income roadmap went, he agreed that I should use an average annual return of just 5% for all of the money going into the two other risk buckets. If he does better than that, he and Connie can either enjoy the excess earnings, save it for a rainy day or add it to their eventual legacy.

Without ever decreasing their retirement income after 10-15 years in retirement, using the income allocation roadmap with conservative projections, the plan works. Even when one of them passes away and they lose a Social Security check, they'll only have to drop their spending by 3-4% in order not outlive their money well beyond age 100.

Although this aspect was not part of their retirement income plan, you'll recall they had a major desire to leave a nice legacy to their three children and their church.

Tom and Connie owned their home which was worth about $620,000. But they had refinanced to help pay for two of their parents' long-term care needs and to do some major home remodeling. They had 12 years left of payments to go and the principal and interest portion was $1,250 a month.

To make a long story short, we used a reverse mortgage to pay-off the loan and they used that $1,250 extra cash flow to pay premiums for those 12 years only for a second-to-die life insurance policy. After that, no premiums would be due.

This policy would pay their beneficiaries (their kids) a guaranteed death benefit once they had <u>both</u> passed away.

With Tom being in normal health for a 64 year old and Connie being in very good health, this $1,250 monthly premium would buy them a life insurance policy with a $500,000 guaranteed death benefit.

Both of them felt that the extra $500,000 guaranteed legacy was more important to them than the tax deduction on the mortgage interest (which gets lower each year as the mortgage is paid down anyway). Not only that, but the reverse mortgage also gave them a line of credit for emergencies down the road as well. This additional strategy accomplished multiple goals.

Are you up for just one more client example of an income allocation retirement roadmap? I'll make it short.

Dale is a divorced 65 year old Realtor who wants to work for as long as he can -- since he loves the job. But he wanted me to design a retirement roadmap that would allow him to stop working at age 70 if he chose to. Every year that he would work beyond that would only make the plan better.

At age 70, he'd like me to plan on a $60,000 after-tax income and grow that by 3% each year to fight inflation.

As far as his savings go, he has an IRA with $260,000 in it and Dale is one of those rare folks that I see who has a ROTH IRA with $74,000 in it. He also has a $45,000 brokerage account with a broker that he hasn't heard from in years.

Being in real estate, Dale also owns a foreclosure rental house that he bought in the 1990's that is fully paid for. It's worth about $100,000 now. During the great recession of 2008, it went down in value by about 50%, but now that its value has recovered, he would like to sell it. He says that neighborhood is declining and he'll take his profit... and run. He has not decided on what to do with the sale proceeds and it is not needed for his retirement income roadmap.

By waiting to age 70, his own Social Security checks should be about $43,000 a year. But since he was married for over 10 years, once he reaches age his full retirement age (66 in his case) he will be able to get divorced spousal Social Security benefits from age 66-70. After prompting him to call the Social Security office, it turns out his ex-spousal benefits will be almost $8,000 a year until he turns on his own benefits then.

That's called a filing a "restricted application" for spousal benefits" Since his marriage lasted more than 10 years, he'll get 50% of his ex's Primary Insurance Amount (PIA). He didn't know about that and very much appreciated my help. At $8,000 a year, we added $32,000 to his income over four years.

When asked about his choices for the 3 buckets of risk, he said that, for money he would need to supplement his Social Security checks, he wanted it all in the Principal Protected bucket. Is he a "probability-based" or a "safety-first" guy?

After working on his income allocation plan, I told him that if he used his all of his traditional IRA for that bucket, he could meet his after-tax income goal on just that and Social Security. Those two sources of income alone would take care of his monthly "nut" based on taking free-withdrawals from the FIA until turning-on the lifetime guaranteed income stream.

When he sells the rental property we might use some of those funds rather than taking the free withdrawals, which would give him an even higher lifetime guaranteed income.

Unless he needed it for an emergency, he did not want to touch his ROTH IRA. He wants to leave it to his grandchildren. We put all $74,000 in the moderate risk bucket with our appropriate wealth managers. Sequence of returns risk was not a concern since we had no plans of taking any income from it.

While he is alive, ROTH's do NOT have any Required Minimum Distributions (RMDs) so he never has to touch these funds unless he wants to. Any money left over in the ROTH will be left to the grandchildren. And if they are smart... they will only take RMDs (based on their life expectancies) and they should enjoy decades of a growing tax-free income stream.

Since he is anxious to move that money from the broker, he decided to move those funds to a FIA that I often use for accumulation rather than for guaranteed income.

This annuity probably has a much better chance for growth in the account (but still no chance for market losses) but has no lifetime income guarantees. It's simply a no-market risk accumulation vehicle. Certainly better than a CD nowadays.

The benefit of taking this money out of a taxable account and putting it in a tax-deferred annuity, is he will not get any more 1099 tax forms that he has to pay income taxes on. His growth will compound untaxed, at least until he withdraws money.

By the way, since these funds were taxable, I would have rather put them in an IUL than this annuity (it's better for IRAs) which would offer even more growth potential. But he is has a medical history of recent cancer (in remission now with a great prognosis) which makes him uninsurable right now.

So basically just using his $260,000 IRA in his Principal Protected bucket along with Social Security we'll reach his lifetime income goal of $60,000 after-tax income growing at 3%. As long as he lives, this income is guaranteed (although the increases are not guaranteed). Dale has no sequence of returns risk and no longevity risk as both checks will come in for the rest of his life.

He'll also have funds from the rental property, his ROTH and his accumulation FIA that can be used for special purchases, emergencies and/or for his legacy. This income allocation plan is going to do exactly what he wants it to and with plenty financial resources to spare.

These are just three examples of a retirement income roadmap. There are dozens and dozens more that are as unique as the couples and persons that came to me for help.

In my experience, the number one concern of retirees, is the fear that they will not be able to maintain their lifestyle over a long retirement. In fact, The Employee Benefit Research Institute survey shows that only 1 in 5 investors are very confident they'll have enough money to live comfortably in retirement. That means the other 4 have worries and doubts.

Although there is no "right" answer for everyone, the basic choice for the direction of a retirement income plan is going to be primarily either "probability-based" or "safety-first".

Most, but not all of my personal clients gravitate to the "safety-first" mindset. Even those clients that are primarily "probability-based" want 15%-25% of their retirement savings in the Principal Protected bucket with a guaranteed lifetime income. And they like how I invest in the other 2 risk buckets.

Economists and professors Dr. David Babbel (Wharton) and Dr. Craig Merril (BYU) wrote in 2007: "The tremendous value that annuities provide in retirement seems to be an area where economists agree... and that you should start by covering 100% of your minimum acceptable level of retirement income (your basic expenses) with annuities" (that is not already covered by Social Security and other pension income). That is pretty close to the definition of "safety-first"... although covering 100% is not possible or even practical for many retirees.

The "probability-based" folks will likely do one of these two things: 1) They will take out too much money (based on a bad sequence of returns) which may result in eventually running out of savings or 2) they will take out too little and thereby reduce the retirement lifestyle they could have had. It could boil down to either financial catastrophe... or regret of not enjoying a better lifestyle during retirement. A realistic income allocation plan reduces much of those real concerns.

You might find it interesting that I have never even met Jim, Mary, Tom, Connie or Dale. They live in 3 different states than I do. They had all read one of my other books and then they contacted me to see if I could help them. We worked together over the phone, internet and through the mail. It was easy for them (no trips to my office) and easy for me. It works for the 90% of clients I've never met in some 22 states so far.

Some Fine-Tuning of Income Allocation

There are times when I'll fine-tune the general income allocation planning that was part of the plan. When the client has the resources and willingness to do so, financial moves like the two described below can add a lot of value and an additional layer of safety to the income plan.

The first potential additional refinement is having a 1 or 2 year "income emergency fund". By an income emergency fund, I mean an account that cannot go down in value due to the markets, yet can fund up to 2 years of any non-guaranteed income that may be needed to supplement your Social Security, pensions and any FIA income.

When markets go down, I'd rather use that emergency cash to replace any income that we were planning to get from the low or moderate risk buckets. Rather than having to sell investments in those two buckets when prices are low, you use your cash emergency fund instead.

The reasoning behind this strategy is that once you sell an asset in a market crash, that asset can never recover in the eventual rebound... since you spent it.

When the markets do rebound, we sell some of those investments in the low & moderate risk buckets to replace the cash we used to supplement the retirement income during the market crash or recession. We try to never sell assets when prices are down to fund our ongoing income needs.

This is another way that I try to reduce sequence of returns risk and help ensure clients do not outlive your money due to a deep or prolonged bear market.

As you know, my clients chose our third party private wealth managers for all or part of those two risk buckets. Taken together, they have the goal of avoiding much of the market losses. But they are not perfect and there is always going to be some drawdown in these portfolios.

I believe these drawdowns may be likely to be less than the ones most "buy, hold, hope...and pray" investors will face, but pas performance is no guarantee of future results

Clients who do not have an outside income emergency fund for times like these, we would recommend the managers that held up the best (or even profited from the market's fall) and let the other manager strategies recover. You could do the same with your own stocks or mutual funds. .

Most advisors who use this type of advanced income planning, use CD's or money market funds. That will work, but in these times of historically low interest, we strive to do better. Your money can (and should) work harder for you.

My favorite cash alternative is an over-funded cash-value life insurance. Now there are times when I'd prefer whole life insurance and other times, when I think an IUL would work best. Some situations call for a single-premium policy while others lend themselves to paying premiums over 5-10 years.

Just like using funds from a bank, the life policy would be

the source of emergency income needed through withdrawals or policy loans. A reverse mortgage HECM (line of credit) is also an excellent choice for this strategy.

The advantage of using life insurance is that we get much higher returns than at a bank and we get the extra protection of the death benefit (of course the life insurance benefit comes at a cost – but you get something very valuable in return for this cost). And some policies offer potential long-term care benefits – using part of the death benefit while you are alive.

While I'm on the subject of life insurance, I'd like to veer off-course for just a minute, OK? Do you already own a cash-value life insurance policy? You may have a whole life or some type of universal life insurance policy in force already. The TV "financial advisors" who say you don't need it, are dead wrong.

What about two Social security checks going to one or a 25%-100% reduction in a pension at the death of a spouse?

If you are fortunate enough to have a life policy, even though you're older now, it sometimes makes absolute financial sense to do a tax-free exchange (1035X) from the old kinds of policies to a new one which has lower mortality costs due to the fact that we are living longer than decades ago - whether your policy is fully paid-up, or you are still paying premiums.

For some strange reason, life insurance is the only industry that tries to keep people from "trading in" their obsolete products for a newer, improved version. Maybe it's time for a policy upgrade. It should certainly be considered as part of a comprehensive financial plan, don't you think?

The internal insurance costs in all life insurance policies are largely determined by the CSO mortality table used at the time of purchase. But over the years as our longevity has increased, these mortality tables have changed – getting a lot less expensive (by up to 30% to 50% or more).

In 2009 and beyond, all life policies MUST be issued using the 2001 CSO mortality tables. Any policy issued before 2001 (and even up through 2008) is burdened with old, outdated life expectancy mortality costs (1980 CSO mortality rates). And if your policy was issued prior to 1980, those CSO mortality costs (set back in 1958) are another 30% more expensive.

A new IUL (or even a new whole life policy) can have much less expensive internal mortality costs (using the latest and least expensive CSO life expectancy tables due to increasing longevity in the USA) even though you are older now.

The bottom line is that your current life policy is likely costing you too much... even if you are no longer making premium payments (either the policy is fully paid-up or premiums are being paid out of the policy cash values or from dividends).

You can possibly get a much larger death benefit, stop future premium payments... or get a new policy with enhanced tax-free Long-Term Care benefits at no out-of-pocket cost to you.

You can even get more tax-free income to supplement your retirement lifestyle if income is a bigger goal than death benefit or potential long-term care benefits. Plus with an IUL, you have the opportunity to earn up to 12%-13% when markets do well.

The average annual IUL interest credited over the last 25 years would have been +7.3%. In fact, the average annual returns during "ANY 15 or 20 or 25 or 30 year period" since 1930 were all over +7%. That's pretty impressive considering there is no stock market risk.

Why settle for a low fixed interest rate return (or stock market risks and volatility in a variable universal life policy) when you can have the opportunity to get both a fixed interest rate or an index strategy (or a combination of the two).

You just need to have your current policy carefully analyzed and see what may be best for you now. Based on my many years of experience, you'll very likely be very pleased with the policy analysis and your potential options to make improvements. There is no cost, so you have nothing to lose.

Let's make sure that any of your existing life policies are pulling their own weight and that you and your family would not be better served with a brand new one.

If you would like, my team does in-depth life insurance "audits" every month for seniors at no cost and without any obligation. Just let me now if you are interested. No medical exam is needed to do our initial due diligence report. If the audit results show that you're a likely candidate for a much improved policy (larger death benefit, lower premiums LTC benefits, etc.), then you can decide how you'd like to proceed.

Reverse Mortgages

OK, let's get back to the second way that I often fine-tune an income allocation plan – either right from the start or at some point during the retirement years, as necessary. When appropriate, a reverse mortgage can be a very powerful financial tool – one that is too powerful to simply ignore.

As these products have become better and better (due to the Reverse Mortgage Stabilization Act of 2013) and are certainly much more consumer friendly, academic researchers (like Dr. Pfau) and many savvy advisors have touted their usefulness and flexibility in retirement income planning.

The problem with most advisors and consumers who categorically refuse to even consider this financial tool, is that they are living in the past. They do not know... what they do not know. They have not kept up with their financial education.

As you know, no financial tool is right for every circumstance. Each and every product or service in any industry has its pros and cons. Nothing is perfect, but a new reverse mortgage offers very flexible options to solve many retirement problems.

According to a LIMRA study, in 1989 only 11% of homeowners aged 65-74 carried a mortgage into their retirement. At that time, the average mortgage balance for these people was about $29,000.

Things are very different today. Almost 44% of people in this age group have a mortgage and the average balance is nearly $137,000.

For some clients, we use a reverse mortgage to pay-off the balance owed on their primary home mortgage. Why consider this? Because if you do not have a monthly mortgage payment (the principal and interest portion), then you do not need as much income to enjoy the same exact lifestyle. You get to live in the same house (for as long as either of you want to) with no more principal and interest payments.

Yes, you'll still have to pay your real estate taxes, HOA dues, homeowners insurance, and maintain the property, but that will always be the case whether your home has a traditional mortgage, a reverse mortgage or is fully paid-off. So in that respect, your ongoing lifestyle (accommodation) is the same. But you just reduced your cost to live (your monthly nut).

Other clients (with their home all or substantially paid-for) can open a HECM reverse mortgage. They get an open line of credit to access the funds whenever they need to or want to. And funds from a reverse mortgage are TAX-FREE. Just like a ROTH distribution or a properly-made distribution from a life insurance policy, funds from a reverse mortgage will not increase your taxation of Social Security.

Or you could use this line of credit to do the same thing as the "emergency cash fund" I described earlier. You could access the line of credit when the markets are falling dramatically rather than selling investments that have dropped in value. And then pay back the line of credit when markets rebound.

Let me give you an example of a 65 year old couple whose home is valued at $250,000 and is paid for. At the time of writing this section, they could establish a reverse mortgage line of credit (that never has to be paid off while they live in the home) of about $127,000. They would have a small amount of closing costs to open a "standby" line of credit but would not owe any loan interest until they actually accessed the money.

Why open the reverse mortgage HECM now, if they don't need the funds today? Well for one thing, the line of credit will increase over time (based on a formula – not appreciation) and it will be available immediately should they ever need the cash.

If untouched, in ten years the line of credit may grow to $190,000. In 20 and 30 years it may grow to $290,000 and $440,000 respectively. Both the growth of the line of credit and interest rates charged on any loans are variable.

Other potential uses, is to tap the reverse mortgage equity line to use as income while your Social Security benefits and other investment accounts grow. One can also take a monthly tax-free income from the reverse mortgage to reduce their portfolio withdrawal rate and sequence of returns risk.

You read earlier about how Tom and Connie are using the saved monthly cash-flow of having the reverse mortgage pay-off their first mortgage to pay for a larger legacy using life insurance. Some folks use the extra cash-flow to purchase long-term care insurance. The potential uses of a reverse mortgage are wide and varied.

You should know that reverse mortgages are non-recourse loans which means, that you or your heirs can never owe more than the home is worth – even if the loan becomes larger than the home's value. That "worry" continues to be a big myth!

If the home is worth more than the outstanding loan balance when the home is sold, then you or your heirs get to keep the rest of any equity.

The home must be your primary residence, must own their home outright or use the proceeds of the reverse mortgage to pay off their existing mortgage. The youngest borrower (spouse) must be at least age 62. Although, a non-borrowing spouse may be younger than age 62.

Many financial advisors (including myself) used to hold the reverse mortgage as a "Plan B". But I've learned that is not the best advice. The best general advice is to open up the HECM line of credit earlier rather than later, and let it grow.

VITAL: Besides the value of your home, in determining the maximum amount of a reverse mortgage you can get, it is NOT your age(s) that is the biggest factor... it is interest rates. The lower interest rates are, the higher the potential line of credit that can be available. If mortgage rates continue to rise, now is an optimal time to explore opening up a HECM line of credit.

Speaking of home values, a HECM line of credit is also a nice hedge against falling house values. Once your line of credit is open, unlike a traditional HELOC, it cannot be decreased or closed – EVER. In fact it grows each year when left untouched. If you home is worth $600,000 and your age is 66 and current interest rates allow a $265,000 HECM. If we have another housing crisis like in the late 2000's, that figure is protected!

Again, no financial tool is perfect or right for everyone, but a reverse mortgage can incorporate your home equity into improving your overall retirement income strategy. Having said all of that, you should know that there are still abuses in the reverse mortgage market. Some mortgage brokers are selling some people a mortgage that is not in their best interest. Or one with maximum costs and fees.

And please, NEVER use the proceeds from a reverse mortgage to make an "investment" in anything. Not an FIA or a mutual fund or anything. That is a regulatory RED FLAG.

Although I do not personally market reverse mortgages to anyone nor get any kickbacks, commissions, fees or any other type of compensation from reverse mortgages, I recommend a fellow Certified Financial Planner™ who has made reverse mortgages her one and only career. She and her team specialize in this niche market and can save my clients costs. Of course, I would still encourage you to shop around and compare. Enough on reverse mortgages.

There are other tweaks and improvements that I make for many client income allocation plans but those are the two ones that come up most frequently. No two income plans are the same just like no two people are the same. Each plan is unique due to different financial circumstances and retirement goals.

Again, distribution planning is all about using the right amount of dollars in the right risk and tax buckets in order to exploit all of your assets in order to maximize lifetime income.

And as I've written, these lifetime retirement income plans are never, "set it and forget it". They are living, breathing plans that are updated and changed as necessary every single year.

For the rest of this book, I'll write about some things that I believe are important to know about that didn't come up in the three income allocation examples above. Knowing if, when and how to use other strategies and financial products is a real value add for anyone going into retirement.

In-Service Withdrawals

In any type of planning, the earlier you get started the more options you have. Not only that, but as I mentioned earlier regarding FIA's, the longer the funds are in the annuity, the higher the initial guaranteed lifetime payout will be.

That can mean one of two things to you. One, you wouldn't need to put as much money in the FIA in order to get the same guaranteed income as you would if you waited until retirement to invest. Or two, you can put the same investment into the FIA earlier and get a larger guaranteed lifetime income.

You can use an IRA (any type) or non-qualified assets such as a brokerage account, savings, sale of property, inheritance, etc. to fund an FIA - but the earlier, the better.

But for most folks, the bulk of their savings is in their retirement plan at work. So here is a way, that not enough people know about to move funds from the low and moderate risk buckets to the Principal Protected bucket with a guaranteed lifetime income for one or both spouses.

Are you over age 59.5 and contributing to your 401k, 403b or TSP plan at work? If so, do you know that 10,000's of employer retirement plans allow you to roll over your balance directly into an IRA while you are STILL contributing to your work plan?

It's called an "in-service withdrawal' and although it's not mandatory that your employer plan allows this, virtually all do. A quick call to your HR department will let you know exactly what your plan rules are.

In addition to funding an FIA, why might you consider doing this for even the other two risk buckets? Well an IRA can allow you to get professional advice, offer more diversification, better investment choices and maybe at a lower cost. You could also reduce the possibility of suffering market losses as you near retirement – the Retirement Red Zone.

It is important to know that even if you do an in-service withdrawal on all or part of your employer plan balance, you can still contribute part of your salary to the plan just as before... and you will still get the company match on your ongoing contributions too.

Many folks who can do so, move all or part of their employer account balances. They move the funds at their plan at work, in hopes to make their accumulated balance work much harder for them – especially if they want it to go into the Principal Protected bucket with guaranteed lifetime income benefits.

Whatever risk buckets you'd like your savings in, let's take a closer look at some reasons why. The same reasoning holds true for 401(k) plans at a former employer too.

Seven Advantages of an IRA... Over a 401(k)

You are likely to agree that 401(k)s and IRA's have many similarities. They are both retirement plans. Both plans can help you lower your tax bill today, provide tax-deferred growth and help provide a taxable income source in retirement. They are both what the IRS calls "qualified plans".

Although long-time followers of my financial philosophy will know that tax-deferred is just a nicer way to say "tax-postponed"! It's possible you will NEVER SAVE any taxes with either one – you only postpone both the calculation of taxes and the payment of the tax.

Will tax rates be higher? What will tax brackets be then and what will be the future cash amount of the eventual payment of the tax owed. Tax "qualified plans" are a growing tax liability that must eventually be paid (balloon mortgage).

But there are also some substantial differences between 401(k)s and IRA's. Some are small and probably won't impact you much, but other differences, in my opinion, can make one type of account far superior to the other. With that in mind, let's explore seven things you can do with an IRA that you cannot do with a 401(k):

1) Have virtually unlimited investment choices.

Most 401k plans may have 2-3 dozen mutual funds or ETF's to choose from. A rare few have 100 funds or more. But an IRA can be invested in some 20,000 of stocks, bonds, mutual funds, IUT's, ETF's, SMA's, annuities, CDs, etc.

2) Get a GUARANTEED lifetime income.

Many of my clients (both young and old) are pretty risk adverse after the market's 50% drops in 2000-2002 and in 2007-2009. They are also feeing like after over seven years without stock market declines, that we aren't too far off from the a possible recession… or bear market drop of 20% or more.

Most 401(k)'s have NO investment choices that offers a guaranteed lifetime income (for either just the employee or to include the lifetime of their spouse too). The only investment choice that can do that is an annuity.

The annuities that I recommend to my clients that want some money in their "Principal Protected" bucket, not only offer a guaranteed lifetime income with no market risk, but an income that will very likely grow most years during a 30+ yearlong retirement.

3) Take a Taxable Distribution Whenever You'd Like.

But beware. They call it a retirement account for a good reason. It's supposed to be for your retirement! But life happens and sometimes people need to access their funds before retirement.

If you are still working for the company sponsoring your 401(k) and you need some additional money, you are at the mercy of your company's plan rules as well as the IRS Tax Code, when it comes to being able to access your money. Each 401(k) plan is different as to what loan provisions, if any, will be available to current employees.

Typically, access to YOUR funds is extremely limited, especially if you're still under age 59 ½. In such cases, you may be able to take a loan from your 401(k) and you may be able to take a "hardship" distribution, but neither of those options is guaranteed to you under the law.

By law, when available under the plan rules, loans are limited to 50% of the value of your account with a maximum loan amount of $50,000.

But with an IRA, you can typically take a distribution from your account whenever you want. There are no legal restrictions. Of course, as noted above, if you take a distribution from your plan or your IRA prior to age 59 ½, you will generally owe income taxes plus a 10% penalty, but if you really need those funds you may not have any other choices.

4) Take Distribution for Higher Education Expenses – Without a Penalty

Generally, distributions taken from a retirement account prior to age 59 ½ are subject to income tax and an additional 10% early distribution penalty. But the tax code does provide for some exceptions to the rules.

One of these exceptions is available if you use your IRA to pay for higher education expenses (college tuition, books, required supplies, a computer for school) for yourself or certain other family members.

Note that this exception is only available if you take money out of an IRA prior to age 59 ½. There is no similar rule for a 401(k).

5) Avoid IRS Tax Withholding

Remember that all qualified accounts (IRA, 401k's, 403b's, etc.) are only "tax-postponed". Paying income taxes is not an option. It's a requirement.

When you take a distribution from your IRA, you can opt out entirely of withholding. This, however, would not be the case if you had a 401(k). Generally, distributions from 401(k)s are subject to mandatory withholding of 20%. There is no opt-out provision.

6) Combine RMDs Between Multiple IRA Accounts

It is not uncommon for people to have several 401(k)s or similar plans accumulated over time through work with different employers. Similarly, many retirees have more than one IRA account. But here is the difference.

If you have more than one 401(k) and you're age 70 ½ or older, you must calculate the RMD for each of those 401(k) plans separately and you must take those RMDs separately from each plan.

However, if you have more than one IRA and you are 70 ½ or older, there is still an RMD that must be calculated for each IRA. BUT if you want to, you can combine the RMDs and take them from any one IRA or any combination of IRAs you so choose without a penalty.

If you did the same thing with your 401(k) plans, you would be subject to a 50% penalty. That is true – for each 401K plan from which you did not take the correct distribution you would pay a huge penalty. Most folks have no idea of this landmine.

7)   Make a Direct Qualified Charitable Distribution

This advantage only applies to people who do not need to

take an income from their IRA in order to pay for their lifestyle and who also make annual contributions to charity.

Qualified Charitable Distributions (QCDs), allow IRA owners and IRA beneficiaries age 70 ½ or older to send as much as $100,000 from their IRA account directly to a charity and not include any of that donation amount in their income on their IRS tax forms.

If you make a QCD, you do not get a charitable deduction, but you never added that income to your tax return in the first place. That can result in a lower tax bill than if you had taken a "normal" IRA distribution and then made a "regular" charitable donation. Plus a QCD can be used to offset all or a portion of your required minimum distribution (RMD).

So those are seven things you can do with an IRA that you cannot do with a 401(k). And you don't have to be retired or not working for your old employer to rollover a 401(k) to an IRA. If you are aged 59.5 or older most 401(k) plans will allow for an "in-service withdrawal" WHILE you are still working at the company… and still contributing (and getting any company match) to your plan!

That doesn't mean that IRAs are better than 401(k)s. They are different. In most cases, for the reasons described above, I prefer my client's retirement money to rollover into an IRA from their current or former 401(k) plan when possible. However, for a few folks, 401(k)'s may be better. For example, you can never take a loan from any IRA account. But you can never take a loan from a former 401(k) plan (you no longer work for the company) – so that's the same rule as with an IRA. And sometimes, 401(k)'s have lower costs than an IRA.

Rule of 100

Back in the late 1990s when I was taking the coursework to prepare for the Certified Financial Planner exam (a 10 hour exam over 2 days which less than 60% usually pass the first time), there was a common rule of thumb called the "Rule of 100".

Basically this rule says that you subtract your age from 100 and the number that results in that simple calculation is the percentage of your investments that you should allocate to stocks. So a 70 year old should have 30% of their investments in stocks and the rest in fixed income (typically bonds).

Given my long held belief that inflation risk was a large retirement risk everyone must face, I never thought much of this rule of thumb. I basically thumbed my nose at it, so to speak, as someone living 20-30 years with so much in bonds was going to lose a war against inflation. I feel even more strongly against this rule now that the end of the 30 year bubble in bond prices is coming to an abrupt end.

Despite sequence of returns risk, equities, real estate and perhaps commodities could be much better hedges against high inflation than fixed income.

And we've already discussed how to remove a great deal of sequence of returns risk with Social Security filing strategies, private money managers and FIAs.

But with today's extremely low bond rates, someone buying a US Treasury 10 year bond now, is locking in an awful low interest rate – about 2.5%. Although the government says that CPI (Consumer Price Inflation) is low, we all know that it is higher than 2.5% in the "real world".

In fact as I originally wrote this section, Switzerland was selling 50 year government bonds for a slightly negative interest rate. Investors are locking in a guaranteed negative return for the next 50 years. Would you invest in that?

The Rule of 100 is a thing of past. Here's a further explanation of why I think you should stay clear of that "rule".

Bonds Are DEAD Money

Bonds certainly have a place in your portfolio. Even the wealth managers in my low risk bucket use bonds in their investment strategies (although not buy and hold), so please understand this section in that light. But here is the bigger case against bonds (and certainly the Rule of 100).

Most professional investors and academics believe that it is only a matter of time before interest rates begin to rise to more normal levels. But truth be told, I and most others have been wrong on the timing of this.

As I update this book, and the Presidential election results are in, interest rates seem to be finally rising, as I and many other people believed would eventually happen.

My timing may have been off, but after the government has been printing trillions of dollars, inflation and interest rates seem to be headed higher (and bond prices lower). Here's a video script from a BLOG post from my website that I wrote in

July 2015. As I said, my prediction was (and still is) too early.

"After a 35 year long bull market in bonds, the time for buying and holding bonds in a 60/40 or 75/25 portfolio mix of stocks and bonds is probably over. Now that is a bold opinion for sure, but stick with me for a minute.

As you probably know, when interest rates GO UP, bond prices GO DOWN. Interest rates and bond process have an inverse relationship. Yields on 10 year US Treasury bonds have DROPPED from 16% in 1981 to a low of 1.6% in March 2015, so the tailwinds have been behind bond prices.

Now (Dec. 2016) they're yielding about 2.5%. So if you believe, like many professionals do, that it's only a matter of time before yields rise to more normal levels of 4-6%, the investors holding bonds bought in the last 6 years are going to LOSE money if they sell their bonds before they mature.

Even if you hold on to them, the values on your account statements will show losses. Aren't bonds supposed to add some stability to your investment portfolio? Yes and they do. Stocks are usually more volatile, but bondholders are in for price decreases (maybe big) should interest rates rise.

You could always go to cash instead, but CD's and money market funds pay hardly anything, and you could slowly LOSE purchasing power. So what does a retiree or near-retiree do?

A person who doesn't want, and shouldn't have too much in stocks? What is a good "bond substitute" where your "protected money" can never lose its value due to the markets, yet earn a reasonable return? A place where your account value WILL NOT decrease at all: no matter what happens in the economy, the stock market, OR if interest rates rise. And where you don't pay taxes until you actually withdraw money!

And unlike bonds, what if those funds would pay you a very competitive guaranteed income stream that you and your spouse can never outlive. It's much better than a pension since you keep control of the money. And unlike most pensions, your initial guaranteed income can potentially double over your retirement years."

So that was my video script. Of course I was describing an FIA as a bond alternative. Not only do bonds face interest rate risk, all except Treasuries, face default risk. And all bonds (except TIPs) face inflation risk as the principal you get back at maturity will buy much less in goods and services.

As this book is winding down, I'd like to leave you with a few miscellaneous thoughts about retirement income planning and a few advanced planning strategies that too many people do not know about.

I started this book (page 18) writing about the major retirement risks that affect just about everyone: longevity, market risk, higher taxes, inflation and rising health care costs.

And if our country and the world experience a low interest rate environment again, that should be added to the risks as well. Extended periods of extremely low interest rates adversely affect all savers and pensioners. But in my own practice, and in those of many of my peers, we routinely run into 5 other retirement risks which I'll write about next.

5 "Not-So Uncommon" Reasons
for Retirement Failure

What is retirement failure? By retirement failure, I mean what would have been a prosperous and predictable retirement... becomes much less so to say the least. Some folks think that we are really richer than they are --- if only because none of us can know what the future holds.

But here are 5 other not-so uncommon reasons why clients can "fail" in retirement. You could also consider them causes of major disruptions to retirement success.

A few of the reasons we have complete control over while others we may have some control over. And we might each come up with different ideas on which ones are which.

But in any case, here we go with some food for thought based on my own professional experiences and those of other financial planners that I keep in close contact with. Here they are in no particular order:

1) Divorce. Divorce rates for those in their 50's and 60's are soaring to all-time highs. In fact, about 25% of all divorces in 2010 were of couples over age 50. Divorce splits assets and income and the effects of this decision is probably clear to all but the very wealthy. I know first-hand, as I was divorced once.

2) Ongoing financial support for adult children (age 30+).
Let them go before they suck your finances dry.

It's time to seriously consider to stop supporting and perhaps enabling our grown kids by keeping them financially afloat and dependent on you. Some call it "tough love".

Another situation that I see all of the time is when the parents feel the need to "fund a new business" for the adult child. If a bank, with all of their billions in assets, that are in the business of loaning money to businesses, won't take a chance on your child, it's probably a great indication that you -- with just millions (or much less). Perhaps you shouldn't take the capital risk with your retirement either.

Sometimes my clients use me as the "bad guy" to simply explain to the adult child(ren) that the parent cannot continue this ongoing financial support or act as a second pair of eyes for the proposed "business plan". Of course, I am not referring to special needs adult children in this discussion. That is a parental responsibility, not a hand-out.

3) Buying a new second (or third) home. Even if the primary home is paid for, the upkeep, maintenance, taxes, insurance on two homes can strain the finances on all but the well-off, once many folks are on a "fixed" retirement income. I often find that the 2nd home becomes a burden over time as expenses rise faster than income during retirement. Just something to think about -- especially if you're not wealthy.

4) Starting a Business. Many clients who have been successful in their careers (especially when they retire early) feel the need to get "back in the game". If you want to start a business - one without a significant capital commitment (such as consulting, real estate agent) that could be a wonderful thing.

However, until it's up and running I wouldn't count on big paychecks from it as part of a long term retirement income stream. If it is successful, then great -- you can add to your lifestyle, savings or legacy.

But I've seen too many IRA's greatly depleted feeding a negative cash-flow business. At the very least, please know a figure at which you will "pull the plug" and cap your losses.

5) Medical Expenses and LTC. Every year the mutual fund family (Fidelity) does a study to project potential health care costs that are NOT covered by Medicare (premiums, co-pays, deductibles, etc.) and in 2016 that number was $260,000 for a couple retiring at age 65. And that figure does not include potential LTC costs - which could add many $100,000's or could be nothing at all.

I realize that health care costs were one of the top five retirement risks described early in the book and it is always the elephant in the room – especially potential LTC costs. I haven't written much about planning ahead for potential long term care costs in this book. Helping folks do this is how I got started in the financial services business in 1997.

Besides a spouse dying too soon (without enough life insurance), a long-term care event is going to be the biggest reason an otherwise "perfect" income allocation plan might fail. Having said that, a "safety-first" income allocation plan can be far superior to the 4% withdrawal "probability-based" plan that so many other folks are just hoping will work. That is because there is less sequence of return risk and longevity risk. But neither philosophy protects against LTC or early death.

The wealthy can self-fund this risk, although I would suggest there are more efficient ways for them to do this than they might be planning on. For the rest of us, there are traditional long term care policies. These have gotten much more expensive over the years and harder to medically qualify for.

Not only that, but there is the "if you never need care, you lose all of the premiums paid" objection. It's a valid one, but that is the way most insurance works. Nobody gets mad that their home doesn't burn down and they never got any monetary benefit from their homeowner's insurance policy.

I've gone from helping 3-5 families a week with traditional LTC policies back in the late 1990's to 3-5 families a year now. That's a huge shift.

There are also life insurance/LTC and annuity/LTC combo products, which do not offer as rich a potential LTC benefit as traditional LTC policies, but either you or your heirs will get something out of the premiums paid – whether you ever have an LTC claim or not. And with most of these combo products, there are no premium increases at all.

While sales of traditional LTC have slowed down markedly over the last five years, sales of these combo products are seeing huge increases – in my practice as well.

I realize that the first 4 of the 5 "not-so uncommon" reasons for retirement failure is not going to be relevant for all readers, but if it helps just a few dozen folks not making an avoidable financial mistake, then I hope the rest of you will forgive me. Everyone needs some sort of plan for potential LTC expenses.

Lazy Money

What is lazy money? It's money that is not earning its keep. Money that can work harder for you over the long term. The types of money that comes to mind first is bank CDs, money market funds, savings accounts plus T-Bills and 2-5 year Treasury bonds. There are literally trillions and trillions of dollars of lazy money sitting at banks alone. There is lazy money everywhere.

There are also billions of dollars more sitting in "outdated" life insurance policies, annuities with no modern income or LTC benefits. Even old and fully matured U.S. savings bonds.

According to Bankrate.com as I write these words, the best 1 year CD rate in the USA right now is 1.26%. The best 3 year CD rate is 1.66%.

And unless they are held inside of an IRA or similar account, that puny interest is taxable each year. You'll get a 1099 tax form from the bank telling the IRS who much interest your earned... and then you'll have to pay the tax. In your mind, even forgetting about paying taxes on any interest earned, are those rates going to keep you ahead of inflation? Probably not.

I realize that the interest rates quoted above are for 1 and 3 year CDs. But what I have found is that many people just roll one CD over into the next – time after time. They may change the term of the next CD but as one CD matures, they just roll it into the next one. I've seen retirees do this for 10 and 20 years or more. Oftentimes, with $100,000's in various CDs at multiple banks with multiple terms.

Now I always recommend my clients have a real emergency fund that is very liquid (within 24 hours) to cover most anything that would come up. Although each person's situation and potential needs are different, I think, ten, twenty or even thirty thousand dollars would meet most retiree's needs.

Reverse mortgages, HELOC lines of credit on your home and unused credit cards also work well for emergencies.

You may recall that earlier in the book, that I compared financial products and services to tools in a toolbox. Another analogy that I often use is to compare them to golf clubs. A putter has a specific purpose and so does a sand wedge and a driver. Even an amateur golfer knows to use the right club for the right situation they face on the golf course.

There are a number of ways to make this lazy money work much harder for us – without taking unreasonable risks. The potential solution for one client may be very different than for another. Again, the goal is the determining factor for which financial tool we use to best meet that goal.

I wrote earlier about having a 1 or 2 year CD alternative for emergency income when the markets are down, there are a few financial "clubs" that would be quite usable in this situation. Other financial clubs would be more appropriate for a LTC combo solution.

Here's a specific example of a "utility golf club" – a financial solution that can solve a number of potential situations, while providing good access to your savings and liquidity.

Simon is a 65 year old in regular health (in fact, a doctor

would likely say a notch or two below that). Besides funds that he has already made available to his income allocation retirement income plan, he had just inherited almost $210,000 after his mother passed away.

He didn't need income from these new funds, but wanted to give some to his four children ($14,000 each since this is the current annual gift tax exclusion amount), give $2,000 to each of his 7 grandchildren, give a nice big charitable donation and take a wonderful three week trip to Europe with his wife Helen, plus add to his emergency fund.

So of the $210,000 or so, he gave $70,000 to his children and grandchildren, made a nice charitable donation, budgeted for his trip and asked me what to do with the leftover $100,000. Of a number of financial options, this was the one that they liked best. I'll summarize it here for simplicity sake.

They put $100,000 into a single premium IUL (life insurance). Based on his age and health, that bought him an $186,000 tax-free death benefit which was a nice extra perk, but he was more concerned about looking for a pretty safe place to grow his money, without income taxation along the way.

This particular IUL is built for accumulation protects much of his single premium (or even increases it) should he need to access the cash in the policy during the first 5 years or so – depending on returns.

This IUL has different indexing options (like most FIAs) but IULs have much higher caps. To make it simple, the S&P 500 index has a cap of 11.5% (the most you can earn with a floor of 1% when the market goes down).

With that cap and floor, the average returns of that index option is over 7.37% for the last 10, 20, 25 and 30 years. So it's not unreasonable to assume that his contract will do better than 7% over the next 10, 15 or 25 years – but there are no guarantees.

For his projections though, I only used an average index crediting gross index returns of 6.5%. At just 6.5%, his cash value would grow from $100,000 to about $140,000 over ten years (net of all insurance costs and policy expenses).

That doesn't sound great (in the first 10 years) at 3.4% per year (tax-deferred) net of all insurance costs, but according to bankrate.com the best five year jumbo CD in the country then was 2.1% (taxable). A 3.4% tax-deferred interest is better than 2.1% taxable and the death benefit is always tax-free to the family.

By the way, the 10 year US Treasury bond was paying under 1.7% and that interest is taxable every year too – and there is NO tax-free death benefit.

Remember that his family is also protected by a growing $186,000 death benefit ($86,000 more than the premium he paid). At age 80 the cash value and death benefit should grow to about $185,000 and $250,000 respectively.

The cash value and death benefit should continue to grow and might become $315,000 and $370,000 respectively at age 90 (at 6.5%). And about $400,000 and $450,000 at age 95, and so on. All with tax-deferral and no stock market risk.

As a point in fact, based on his age and health, the cheapest ten year term life insurance policy would cost $800 a year for $86,000 of death benefit coverage. But that cost (an $8,000 value) is already included in the returns above.

Although this financial club is not a substitute for a life/LTC combo product, Simon does have the option to access part of the death benefit should he qualify for long-term care. If LTC protection was the primary financial goal, we would have chosen a different product (financial club) that was specifically built for that purpose.

Of course if leaving the largest guaranteed tax-free legacy possible to the kids and grandkids were the goal rather than tax-deferred accumulation without market risk, we would use different financial clubs or tools for that financial goal.

I could continue with many little-known financial strategies that might be interesting to a small percentage of you. But let's head for the finish line of the book and wrap it up.

The Two Retirement Doors

Now that you are already retired or close to retiring, are you 100% sure that you are going to have a great retirement, or do you some doubts? Even if one of you live well into your 90's?

It's really pretty simple, whether you lean to "probability-based" or to "safety-first". There is only one potential result. You see, there are only two possible doors to go through at retirement. Door #1: is that your MONEY will outlive you. Door #2: is that YOU will outlive your money! There is NO 3rd door!

There are 10,000 Americans who retire every day. Many of those folks are in deep trouble. Most do not have a written, date specific retirement savings or an income distribution plan. No plan for longevity or inflation risks. What I've been referring to as either an income allocation plan or retirement roadmap.

Most of them fully realize it but they don't know what to do to fix it. Sure, you want to walk through door #1 but do you have a real plan to do so? No matter how long you might live?

Whether you are still saving for retirement, or are currently retired, do you know exactly how much money it is going to take for you to retire comfortably when you want to... and/or for you and your spouse to REMAIN comfortably retired?

We've discussed sequence of returns risk throughout this book and the big difference between saving for accumulation and retirement income distribution. How much market risk do you need to take to get the returns you want to afford you the retirement lifestyle that you've been hoping for decades? Do you know?

Well, a non-scientific answer, but one that most people close-to or already in retirement, can really relate to, would be "as LITTLE risk as necessary".

Here's another way to put this all important retirement question. What potential percentage return is worth hoping to get, to put much of your life savings at risk? Is it for a 20% potential return? A 12%, 9% or maybe a 7% return?

Now we all understand the ratio of risk and reward. The more risk one takes, the higher the potential reward could be. But we know that higher risk means, that not only might we get bigger potential returns, we must also endure and live with a much greater chance of loss... and stress.

Where should you invest the dollars in the two risk buckets to get the highest potential returns with the lowest drawdowns possible? When is a "good time" to lose money?

Most folks need to take some risk in their income allocation plan in order to reach their retirement income goals. So it's not If you take investment risks or not, but how much risk do you need to take to reach your retirement income and legacy goals.

Do you remember the example of the brother and sister, Bill and Jill who retired just three years apart with the same $1,000,000 of assets? Bill's savings grew despite taking the same withdrawals as Jill. Jill just retired 3 years too late.

As far as stock market risk goes, does it make sense to be opportunistic in good times (enjoy the fruits of the market) and defensive in bad times? That's the goal of portfolio managers that will go to cash when things get rough in the markets.

Income Allocation Summary

Nobody wants to "un-retire". If I had to summarize an income allocation plan in its most basic form to get through retirement door #1, here's how it might go.

You take the after-tax income that you are wanting to enjoy in retirement and increase that by an inflation rate. Then you subtract the guaranteed income you'll get from Social Security and pensions. Next, you use enough of your savings to buy an FIA (or perhaps a SPIA) which will give the most or all of the rest of the growing income that you'll need to make your "monthly nut". That's "safety-first".

And finally, the rest of the savings can go into the two other risk buckets to use for major purchases, emergencies, extra fun, more growth potential and a potential legacy (family, charity, etc.).

At its core, the retirement income allocation plan offers as much financial predictability, security and certainty as possible – without any regard to how an advisor gets paid.

It's strategies that matter, not products. There are several tweaks that can be employed to make the plan even more secure and further reduce the top five risks to your retirement.

Your Social Security filing strategy is one. Your situation and filing options are as unique as you are. You've contributed to the system for decades, now it's your turn to make the most of your "earned" benefits. Make your filing decision within the full context of your overall income allocation plan.

So is the wise use of the three tax buckets to reduce taxes and control the timing of them as best as you can. What are you doing now to reduce your income taxes throughout your retirement? What plans have you made to create more tax-free income in retirement? Do you have a plan to move money from the "forever taxed" buckets to the "never taxed" bucket?

Are you, your CPA or financial advisor "managing" your tax brackets? If not, why aren't your current advisors doing this?

Should you consider how or when might you use a reverse mortgage to accomplish your lifetime income goals? It could be another important aspect to "perfect" your income plan.

Collaborative Planning

It is my sincere hope that you have not only enjoyed this book, but you have gained much more insight into planning for your retirement income.

As I wrote in the preface, my purpose here is not to provide a one-stop answer for every near-retiree in America. No book could do that. But my purpose is to give the reader a very broad and encompassing, yet highly easy-to-read resource that will provide you with many different aspects of planning your retirement. I hope this book accomplished this goal.

Most people only retire once. They get one shot to make the best decisions that they can. Some decisions, like filing for Social Security or when, how or if to take a monthly pension vs. a lump sum, etc., offer few opportunities to reverse. Others can be easily changed, albeit at a potential loss. What is the long term cost... of making mistakes?

Again for most of us, retirement success is about a having a dependable and growing cash-flow that will continue for as long as you and your spouse are alive. If we can get most or all of what we need without taking any more market risk than you need to, then all the better.

That's why my practice is more about income allocation instead of the typical asset allocation. A guaranteed and perhaps tax-efficient monthly cash-flow for up to 30-40 years of "unemployment" is the name of the game. When most folks really think about it, it's all that matters in the end.

You've arrived at the peak of Mt. Everest and you are ready to descend. The trip back down the mountain is always the most dangerous part of the journey. That's where the top five retirement risks: longevity, inflation, investment losses, higher health costs and potential tax increases are likely to happen.

World famous speaker and motivator, Tony Robbins, in his 689 page best-selling book, "MONEY Master the Game: 7 Simple Steps to Financial Freedom" which among other topics, stresses the importance of "setting up a lifetime income plan".

In his book he makes a great statement about retirement: "Income... is the <u>outcome</u> that matters". It's really all about dependable cash-flow that gives one financial freedom.

Even though Tony has never designed a retirement plan for anyone, does setting up a lifetime income allocation plan make sense to you? Could you benefit from detailed written plan? If your current financial advisor hasn't done this for you already, why hasn't that happened? Do you have to initiate it?

Should you decide you want professional help in building an income allocation plan, you have three choices. You can choose a fee-<u>only</u> advisor who distains commissionable insurance products (like the guy that "hates annuities... and thinks you should too"). They will never offer you financial products (FIAs and SPIAs) that can do what no other products can do – completely eliminate sequence of returns risk and longevity risk. Guaranteed products... are not in their golf bag.

Because they are adverse to commissions, they will not offer, even when the goal calls for it, life insurance for guaranteeing your legacy goals for family or causes that you are passionate about. Nor using it as a powerful tax-free ROTH IRA alternative.

You can also choose an insurance agent. They either think insurance is the right answer for every financial goal (wrong!) or they are too lazy to get licensed to offer investment advice.

Or you can choose a fee-based investment advisor that offers both investment securities (stocks, mutual funds, ETF, etc.) on a fee basis... and insurance products for financial solutions that only insurance companies can legally provide.

As a fee-based Certified Financial Planner™ and fiduciary, I have a golf bag full of all the necessary golf clubs to enable my clients to easily navigate the toughest courses in the world. In other words, having all of the tools and expertise necessary to reliably meet your retirement income and legacy goals.

Many people want to have a retirement distribution plan. A real personalized, goal-oriented income plan that they can understand, believe and follow for decades.

Collaborative planning or CP for short, is a joint retirement income planning effort between the client and the advisor. The CP process is very simple and most consumers love it.

My clients share their financial information and retirement goals with me. It's 100% confidential whenever you are dealing with a Certified Financial Planner™. From that information and your desired after-tax monthly income, I start to build the income allocation plan using experience and financial software.

The end result is a first draft of your proposed retirement roadmap. It shows a year by year, column by column detailed breakdown of where the desired income is going to come from. It takes into consideration Social Security, pensions, your 3 risk and 3 tax buckets, anticipated life expectancies, tax brackets, conservative rates of returns, and even your legacy goals.

For those folks (usually just about everyone) that wants or needs to have a percentage of their savings in the "Principal Protected" bucket – especially with a guaranteed lifetime income to fully beat longevity risk – we'll look at some FIA options. As I go over the plan with the client, I give them the pros and cons of each idea, product or strategy discussed.

Once they have had the opportunity to study the 1st draft of the plan, they come back with questions and give me the yeses and no's, whether that idea, product or strategy should be included in their income plan. And then I go back to work to get the plan exactly the way they want it and present it again.

When the design is finished, they understand the pros and cons of the entire plan and the client decides whether they will implement all or part of the plan or nothing. I may specialize in income planning, but it's their money, retirement and legacy.

It is their decision... not mine. They gave input through the whole process. That's why I call it collaborative planning. My experience and access to all "financial clubs" meets their goals. I can compare a "probability-based" to a "safety-first" plan. It takes a number of hours, but a true comparison is worth it.

If you prefer a "probability-based" plan, hoping to limit drawdown and having available cash for market downturns is going to be absolutely critical to not outliving your savings. You'll have more risks but you'll get more legacy potential. A well-designed "safety-first" plan provides much more guaranteed income with very little longevity and market risk and with fewer financial worries. That choice is up to you.

As I wrote earlier, either retirement income plan is not a one-time "set-it and forget-it" plan. Every year (and more often if needed) we'll see what happened in the previous year, look at the year ahead and make any adjustments necessary.

I invite my readers to contact me directly if they believe I might add significant value to their retirement planning or have questions about how income allocation can reduce longevity risk, market risk, inflation risks, and perhaps even the risk of higher taxes. It's a 30 plus year cash-flow income plan based not on hopes or dreams, but as much certainty as possible.

I'll take the time to listen and fully understand your situation before I even think responding whether I think I can help you or not. You can determine if what I do and how I do it, fits with what you are looking for in a long-term advisor relationship.

There is no cost, nor any obligation to have a 15-20 minute phone conversation with me to learn more. And if you'd like, I can also show you examples of my written lifetime income plans. Please be patient if I'm not available within 24-48 hours.

But I will not forget about you. Whether you lean towards "probability-based" or to "safety-first", let's speak soon.

About the Author: Mark J. Orr, CFP® RICP®

770-777-8309 Office
mark@SmartFinancialPlanning.com

www.SmartFinancialPlanning.com
12600 Deerfield Parkway Suite #100   Alpharetta, GA 30004

Mark has been a practicing Certified Financial Planner™ since 2000. Certified Financial Planners are held to the strictest ethical and fiduciary standards. He has also earned the year-long Retirement Income Certified Professional® (RICP®) designation. Since 1997, he has held life, health and the Series 7 Securities license and became a Registered Investment Advisor soon thereafter owning his own fee-based firm from 1999-2016.

He is now an Investment Advisor Representative under Horter Investment Management, LLC – through which he manages his clients' stock and bond market based investments – ("Low Risk" and "Moderate Risk" buckets) using lower-risk, lower-volatility private wealth money managers. These accounts are allocated into portfolios based on a client's risk tolerance, tax situation, time horizon, and their income and legacy goals. These money managers focus first on minimizing account drawdown (sequence of returns risk) while capturing as much of the market's upside as possible.

Another main focus of his financial practice is using cash value life insurance for tax-free retirement income (a very attractive alternative to a ROTH IRA with many living-benefits that even ROTHs cannot offer).

He is also the author of "Social Security Income Planning: The Baby Boomers' 2017 Guide to Maximize Your Retirement Benefits" as well as several white papers and eBooks and has led dozens of public seminars on various financial planning and retirement topics. He's been quoted in the USA TODAY as well as being a guest on several morning radio shows across the country.

Prior to the financial services business, Mark spent the early part of his career in the luxury resort real estate development and marketing industry – managing $100 million of sales in Europe over a 7 year period. That was back when that was "real" money -- lol! After that he owned a few franchises and then sold those businesses.

He is a two-time past board member of his Rotary Club and continues to be active in community service through the Rotary Club. On a personal note, Mark and Norma live in Alpharetta, Georgia and love to travel – especially to warm sandy beaches in the sun. Staying in good shape is important to him and he enjoys good red wine. Finally, he is the very proud father of three grown children (Megan, Marina and Michael) and four wonderful grandchildren (so far).

Acknowledgements and Disclosers

I'd like to thank mentors of mine, David Gaylor and Gary Reed, who as far as I know, coined the term, "income allocation". We may look at it a little differently, but the results for the client are the same. I'd also like to thank long-time mentors the EAGLE TEAM, Don Blanton, Drew Horter and David McKnight for teaching me so much over time.

Thank you again for your purchase and for reading my book. I hope that it has opened your eyes to the many wonderful possibilities ahead for you during your retirement!

CPSIA information can be obtained
at www.ICGtesting.com
Printed in the USA
LVOW03s1427090517
533874LV00008B/578/P

9 781535 292788